GW00483039

YOUR BOOK OF AEROMODELLING

The YOUR BOOK Series

Your Book of Aeromodelling
by Robert R. Rodwell

FABER AND FABER

3 Queen Square

London

First Published in 1962
by Faber and Faber Limited
3 Queen Square, London WC1
New and revised edition 1968
Reprinted 1971 and 1975
Printed in Great Britain by
Unwin Brothers Limited
The Gresham Press, Old Woking, Surrey
All rights reserved

ISBN 0 571 04644 4

© 1962 Robert R. Rodwell
revised edition © 1968 Robert R. Rodwell

ACKNOWLEDGEMENTS

Several companies and individuals have helped me considerably in the preparation of this book, both in its original form and in this revised second edition. I must express my gratitude to Keil Kraft Ltd for permission to reproduce the plan of the Cadet glider, and for providing some other illustrations. My thanks are also due to D. Sebel and Co Ltd, and to Electronics Developments Ltd for the "exploded" drawing of the 1.5 c.c. Super Fury diesel engine. Finally, I am indebted to Mr. Reinier Stoop, who made the other drawings, and Mr. Barry Wheeler for some valuable advice.

R.R.R.

CONTENTS

ILLUSTRATIONS

PLATES

between pages 16 *and* 17

11

LINE DIAGRAMS

ILLUSTRATIONS

CHAPTER I

Why aeromodelling is fun

Making your own flying model aircraft is a grand hobby; it is perhaps the finest craft hobby you can practise with little money and without expensive tools. It is a hobby which can occupy you at any time and whatever the conditions; winter evenings or wet weekends can be enjoyably spent in making models but when the sun shines and strong winds give way to gentle breezes there is another kind of enjoyment—the thrill of seeing your models fly; the constant variety in their behaviour from flight to flight, the exhilarating chase to retrieve them.

It is an enthralling hobby, too, for different reasons. By building flying models a whole vast realm of science is open for you to explore. Gradually you will come to learn about many aspects of aviation; the theory of flight, methods by which aircraft are built and flown, how engines work. Between the modest models you make at first, and the fastest and most complex aircraft in the sky today, there are, believe it or not, some fairly strong connections.

The very earliest flying machines were "aerostats"—or lighter-than-air craft. These were nothing more than balloons filled at first with hot air (which is lighter than cold air) and later with hydrogen or coal gas, both of which are also lighter than air. They flew because the weight of air they displaced was more than their own weight; this gave them *buoyancy* and they simply floated in a sea of air.

But far-sighted men soon saw that the aimless, drifting aerostat, at the mercy of the slightest breeze, was no great hope for the future. They thought in terms of heavier-than-air craft, "aerodynes", which would generate lifting forces to keep them in flight by their very passage through the air. Such aircraft could be directed at will, controlled at all times, and would not be at the mercy of the wind.

And when they formed, gropingly, their early theories about how this could be achieved, they turned to models. All the earliest pioneers were experimenting aeromodellers. Sir George Cayley, now universally honoured as "the father of aeronautics", was using heavier-than-air models to prove his theories 150 years ago; Stringfellow, Henderson, Langley and many other pioneers followed him.

Even today, models are still widely used to test new theories, and new ideas. There is scarcely any large-scale project in aeronautics costing many millions of pounds, which does not rely on tests performed with flying models before "the real thing" is built. Scientists and designers are very much aware of their value. There are very few scientists, engineers or pilots prominent in aviation today who did not build flying models in their youth for fun. Many of them still do so for their recreation.

Above all, aeromodelling is a progressive hobby; it can be as simple or as complicated as your skill, time and money will allow. Although you will start by building very simple models which cost only a few shillings or even pence apiece, there is no limit to how complex they can become. Many modellers who only a few years back were building the simple kind of models described in this book are now building and flying impressive radio-controlled models—aircraft which remain under their control even two or three miles away, and which can be made to perform manœuvres "just like the real thing". From the 30 in. wing span glider, the building of which is described in the following pages, you can progress in time to others with wings spanning several feet, which can soar for hours over slopes, under your control.

There is hardly a "real" aircraft flying today which cannot be reproduced with satisfying realism in flying model form, from elegantly lazy sailplanes to the noisiest, fastest jet fighter; from the most spidery of helicopters to the most bulbous of flying boats. Aeromodelling, then, is an engrossing hobby, with rich rewards in interest and sheer fun. But proceed carefully, making sure you learn something all along the way.

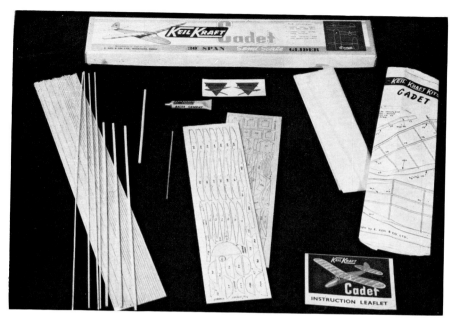

1. The Cadet kit, when opened

2. To begin, the first fuselage side is pinned out . . .

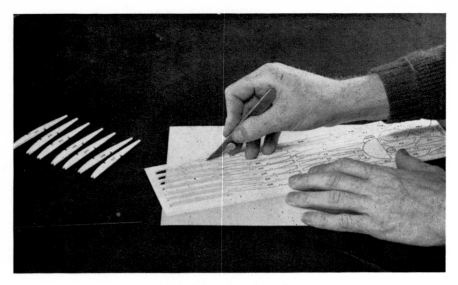

3. . . . and while it dries, the wing ribs are cut out . . .

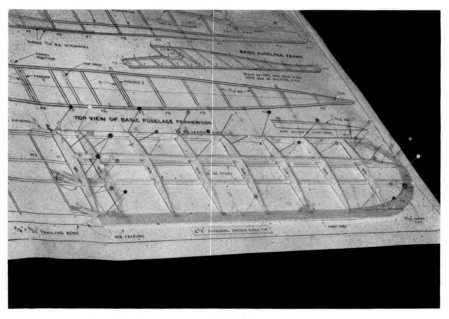

4. . . . for one wing to be built

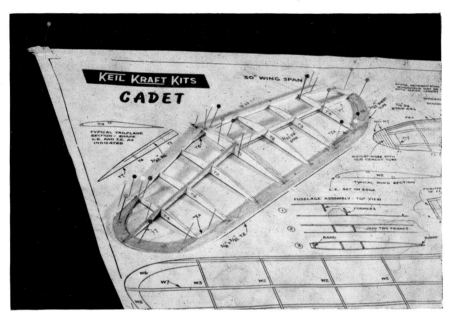

5. The tailplane's structure is similar to that of the wing . . .

6. . . . while the basic fuselage structure is the "box" seen here. Sub-formers
and stringers are soon to improve its appearance

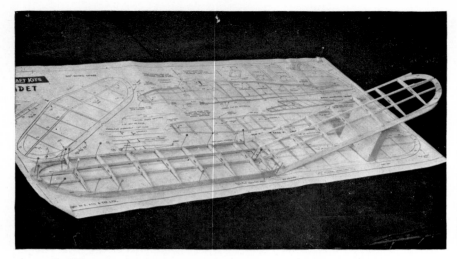

7. When both wings are built, they are joined in a shallow "V" like this . . .

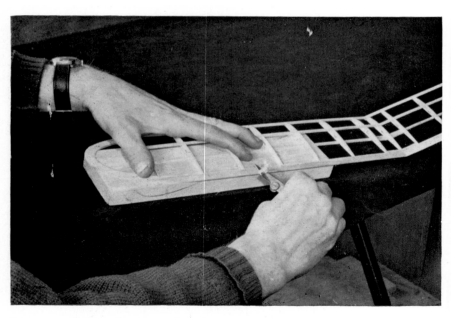

8. . . . and after the centre join has set, the leading and trailing edges are cut and sanded to their proper contours . . .

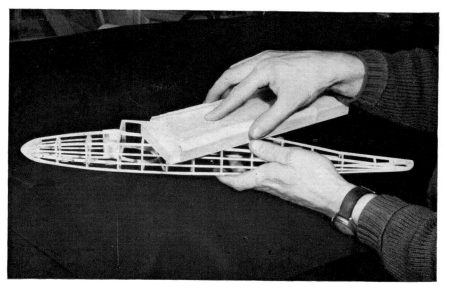

9. . . . gentle sanding completes work on the fuselage . . .

10. . . . and the model is complete, needing only to be covered

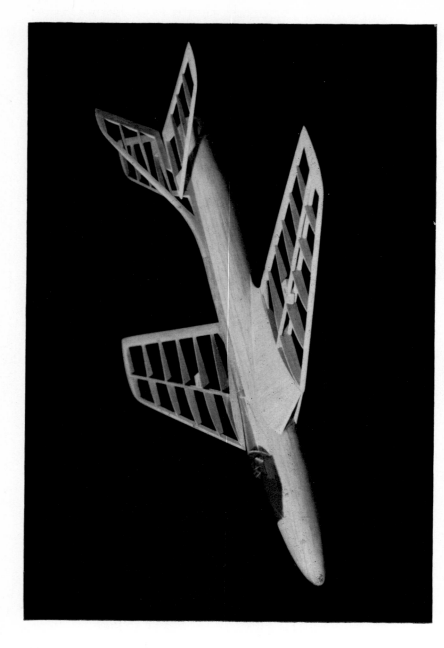

11. A Jetex scale model of the RAF's Hawker Hunter fighter, which will fly in a very realistic manner when complete

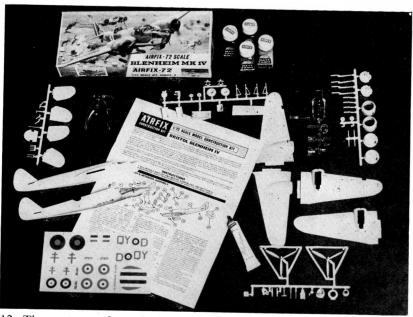

12. The contents of a typical plastic scale model kit, Airfix's 1/72nd-scale Bristol Blenheim IV, a Second World War light bomber

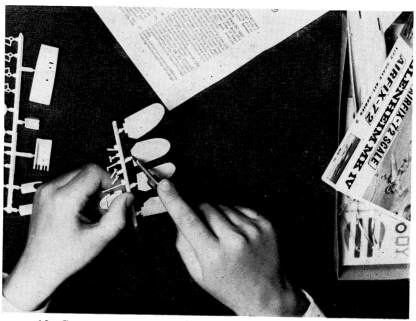

13. Components are attached to plastic stalks and are easily removed . . .

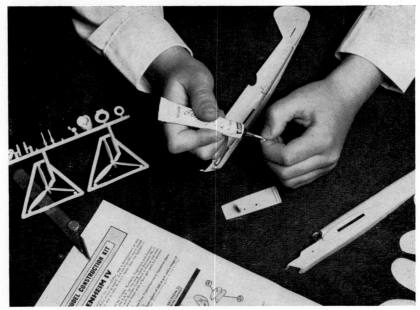

14. . . . for the main fuselage shells to be glued together

15. The wing pressings, top and bottom, are similarly joined, using the cement sparingly . . .

16. . . . and after mating of wings to fuselage, the engine nacelles are prepared. Here a propeller is being mounted

17. When all details are in place, painting begins . . .

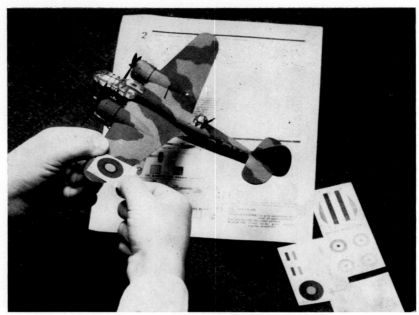

18. . . . and roundels are added, using the transfers provided in the kit

19. With care in assembly and finishing, the results can be superb

CHAPTER 2

Beginning your first model

It is wise to begin aeromodelling by building a simple model glider, and not become discouraged at the start by trying something too complicated. There are several cheap and simple glider kits on sale at most model shops, any one of which will be suitable for your first model. The one shown in the pictures is the KeilKraft Cadet, with a wingspan of 30 in. The kit costs a few shillings. The building methods for this model are the same as those for the smaller gliders on the market and are no more difficult, but being a little larger, its performance is better. Generally speaking, larger models perform better than the smaller ones, and any glider up to about 36 or 40 in. wingspan will be suitable to begin.

Few other things are required. You will need a building board; a smooth, flat and fairly soft piece of wood on which to spread the plan. This need not be as big as the plan, for you can pin different parts of the plan to the board, according to the part you are building, but it must be at least 20 in. long. The plan can be pinned directly to an old kitchen table or work bench if the surface is flat.

You will need a small modelling knife which can be bought at any handicraft shop, or you can use single-edged razor blades, which have a spine along the back by which they can be held. Do not use the thin double-edged razor blades with holes along the middle, as these are brittle and break easily and they cannot be held without the danger of cutting one's fingers. Other things you need to begin are a packet of pins and a light hammer with which they can be tapped into the building board (or more expensive glass-headed pins which can be pushed into the board); a sheet of fine grade sandpaper; four drawing pins to pin down the plan; some greaseproof paper and probably an extra tube of balsa cement, for few of the cheaper kits have sufficient to finish the model.

17

On opening your kit, you will find several thin strips of balsa wood, some sheets of balsa on which the shapes of many parts are printed, some sheets of tissue paper, a few inches of fine wire, a length of hardwood dowel, celluloid (if the model you have chosen is of the realistic kind with a cockpit), a tube of cement and the plan. Spread out your plan and pin it to the building board—if you have only a small building board, pin to it first that part of the plan which shows a side view of the **fuselage**—that is, the body. Cover the plan with transparent greaseproof paper to prevent the structure being glued to the plan over which it is built.

Balsa wood varies greatly in hardness and strength, so before beginning inspect the wood in your kit to see whether it is all of one grade, or several grades. If the strips are both hard and soft—easily determined by pressure of the thumbnail—select the strongest for the **longerons**, the strips which run from nose to tail of the fuselage. You then begin to build the first side frame of the fuselage by pinning these longerons to the plan.

With thin strips, such as the $\frac{3}{32}$ in. square strips with which the Cadet fuselage is built, do not push the pins through the strips, as this will weaken them, but hold the strips in place with the pins placed alternately on either side of the strip, working directly over the plan. With the longerons in place, you are then able to cut the vertical **spacers** to size, and cement them in their places.

Use the softer strips for the spacers, if you have different grades of balsa, and take care when cutting these to size that you cut the ends at the correct angles to butt neatly against the longerons, which are not parallel. The way to do this is to cut each spacer off the strip a little oversize, and then gradually shave the ends until it is just long enough to fit firmly between the longerons at the point indicated for it. Before cementing it into place, use it as a guide to cut a second spacer of exactly the same length, and with its ends similarly angled, and place the second spacer in a box on one side. The set of duplicate spacers will be used when you are making the second fuselage side frame.

Each side frame will contain several pieces cut from the printed balsa sheets. They will be numbered on the plan, F 1, F 2, F 3, and so on, and the appropriate pieces will be numbered on the wood. Cut these pieces out, taking care to hold your knife or razor blade upright so that the wood is cut through squarely. Cut out each pair of fuselage pieces, and compare them against each other, trimming them, with your blade or sandpaper, so that they match exactly. One piece in each pair is then put with the duplicate spacers and the other cemented into place. These shaped pieces can be held in place by fine pins driven through them, without being weakened as strips would be. Spacers will not require pinning into place, for if you have cut them accurately they will fit firmly into place and will not dislodge while the cement is setting.

Do not be too lavish with balsa cement, but guard against using it too sparingly, for a "dry" joint will be a weak one. Ideally, you should apply just enough for some to be squeezed out of the joint when the pieces of balsa are pressed together and the excess should be wiped away. The strongest joints are made by applying balsa cement to both the surfaces being joined, and allowing this first coat a few minutes to dry, without bringing the surfaces together. A second coat is then applied and the joint made. This method of cementing is recommended for the most important joints, but can be used right through the construction. It will take longer, but will be worthwhile in terms of a stronger model.

CHAPTER 3

Making the wings

While the first side frame is setting, you can prepare to make the wings. There will be one or two sheets of balsa in the kit with the **wing ribs** printed on them. These are gently curved pieces, with notches in them for the **spars**—balsa strips which run from wing tip to wing tip.

The performance of your model will depend largely on the accuracy with which you cut out the wing ribs, for the cross section of the wing —called the **aerofoil section**—plays a vital part in generating the *lift* which sustains the aircraft in flight. The aerofoil section will vary in different parts of the wing if the ribs are not exactly the same shape and size and this will adversely affect performance.

Cut out the ribs very carefully following the outside of the printed line. With simple model aircraft you will find that the bottom edges of the ribs are perfectly straight; when you build more complicated, high performance models you will find that both top and bottom edges are cambered. For cutting straight edges you can use a steel rule, or any other hard straight edge, as a guide. Cut out the notches for the spars by making the side cuts and then just pushing out the waste wood with a corner of the razor blade. Make these notches a little narrower than their marked size.

There will be one or two pairs of ribs smaller than all the others. These are used near the tips, where the wings taper. Put these to one side and gather all the other ribs together for sandpapering until they are all exactly the same size. This is best done by pinning them together in one big "sandwich".

To do this hold all the ribs firmly together with the spar notches all in line, pressing the flat underside against the building board. Push in two large pins from one side of the pack to hold them all together—if your pins are not long enough to hold all the ribs, push pins in from both sides.

When you have the ribs pinned together they are ready for sandpapering—lightly! Hold a strip of sandpaper around a small block of wood, or a matchbox, and sand the whole block of ribs, holding the sanding block square to the ribs so as not to take off too much at one side or the other. When you have sanded the surfaces of the block of ribs smooth and before separating the ribs, cut the spar notches to their final size, testing it with a length of $\frac{3}{32}$ in. strip, which should fit firmly into them.

When you have prepared the ribs, you can then cut from the **thicker** sheet the **tip pieces**, marked W 1, W 2 and so on. As you did with the sheet parts for the fuselage, hold each pair firmly together and sand them to match.

It is then time to turn again to the fuselage, to build the second side frame. You do this directly over the first, which you still have pinned to the plan. To prevent the second side sticking to the first, some modellers place small squares of greaseproof paper between them at each joint, but this is not really necessary. It is quite easy to separate them with a razor blade after they are both lifted from the plan.

The second side is built in exactly the same fashion as the first, using the duplicate set of spacers which you cut and placed to one side. Take care to select the right strips for the longerons; this should match in hardness the wood used for longerons in the first. These are threaded between the pins which hold their shape and the spacers and shaped parts are cemented in place immediately above their partners in the first side frame.

The two main **formers**, which are drawn on the plan, should then be made from $\frac{3}{16}$ in. wide strip and shaped parts cut from sheet. These two formers, X and Y, hold the two side frames apart at the front and rear of the wing mounting.

While the second side frame and the two built-up formers are setting, make the **fin**, the upright part of the tail. The fin is a simple structure of shaped parts cut from sheet balsa, marked R 1, R 2 and so on, and $\frac{3}{32}$ in. square strip. Simply cut out the sheet parts, and pin them to the board, cementing them where they join. Apply pins to both sides of the joints to hold them under pressure while the cement sets. Pin out the piece of strip which makes the front edge—called the **leading edge**—cementing this at top and bottom where it joins the sheet parts. Cut it at the top so that the smooth curve of the tip is continued to the front. Then cement in the fin ribs, also cut off $\frac{3}{32}$ in. strip, notching these into the sheet parts which make the rear edge, called the **trailing edge**.

While this is setting you can cut the remaining printed parts. These are the ribs and tip parts for the **tailplane**. The Cadet has a tapering tailplane, so there are only two ribs of each size. When these are cut out, match the pairs, holding them tightly together while lightly sanding their edges so that they match.

By the time you have done this you can lift the fuselage sides and fin from the plan, to move another part of the plan on to the building board, if the latter is small, and build the first wing. It does not matter which one you make first, left or right—or in proper aeronautical language, **port** or **starboard**.

The trailing edge of the wings is a wide strip—in the Cadet seen in the photographs it is $\frac{3}{8}$ in. wide by $\frac{3}{32}$ in. thick. Pin out the first trailing edge, taking care not to put in any of these pins along the inside edge exactly where the ribs are to go. Do not cut off the strip exactly where the wing centre line is marked, but leave an inch or so to spare.

The ribs are notched into the trailing edge, so before proceeding any further you must make the notches. Using a sharp razor blade, and looking down directly over the plan, make small incisions, $\frac{1}{16}$ in. apart, and projecting about $\frac{1}{8}$ in. into the trailing edge. Make these pairs of small cuts where every rib is marked, and then remove the tiny piece of wood between them with a pin.

The Cadet wings have two spars, between the leading and trailing edges, and of these, the rear one is on the undersurface. Pin a piece of hard $\frac{3}{32}$ in. square strip where this is marked along the plan, again leaving an inch or so spare at the centre, but cutting it off exactly where indicated at the tip. You are then ready to cement the ribs into the notches in the trailing edge and to the spar, making sure that they are set squarely to both.

Another $\frac{3}{32}$ in. square strip is then cemented in place to make the leading edge. Placed corner-down to the plan, this fits into the "vee"-

shaped notches cut in the front (the **nose**) of the ribs, and is held in place with pins set along the front. The wing tip pieces, which have earlier been cut from $\frac{3}{32}$ in. sheet and the edges carefully sanded, can then be cemented in place in the same manner as you built up part of the fin from similar pieces. Do not spare the cement, and ensure that you have good joints between the tip pieces themselves, and where they join the leading and trailing edges.

One of the sheet tip pieces is set edge-on to the plan, and cemented between the tip and the end rib. (This is numbered W 7 on the Cadet.) At its rib end this will have a notch along the top surface in which fits the top spar, which can now be put in place. Again, remember to leave an inch or more to spare at the centre end.

Finally, cement in place the centre rib, which is cut of thicker sheet than the others. This must be set at a slope to the board, for the two wings will be cemented to each other in a shallow "vee", and the rib will then be upright. You can obtain the correct slope with a small template—a guide—which is marked on the printed sheet balsa.

One wing is now virtually complete.

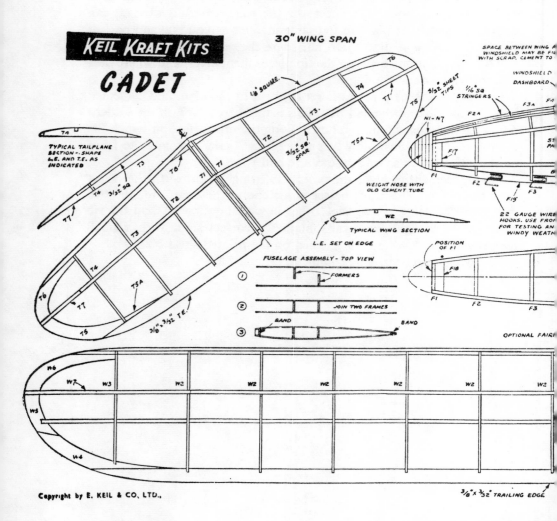

KEIL KRAFT KITS

CADET

30" WING SPAN

TYPICAL TAILPLANE
SECTION - SHAPE
L.E. AND T.E. AS
INDICATED

1/8 SQUARE.

3/32" SHEET
TIPS

3/32" SQ.
SPAR

WEIGHT NOSE WITH
OLD CEMENT TUBE

T4
T5
T6
T7
T5A
T3
T2
T1
T8

3/16" × 3/32" T.E.

TYPICAL WING SECTION

L.E. SET ON EDGE

WE

FUSELAGE ASSEMBLY - TOP VIEW

① ⎯ FORMERS

② ⎯ JOIN TWO FRAMES

③ BAND   BAND

SPACE BETWEEN WING
WINDSHIELD MAY BE FI
WITH SCRAP. CEMENT TO

WINDSHIELD
DASHBOARD

1/16" SQ.
STRINGERS

NI - N7

F17

F1

F2

F19

F3

F2A

F3A

F4

ST
PA

POSITION
OF F1

F18

F1   F2   F3

22 GAUGE WIRE
HOOKS. USE FROM
FOR TESTING AN
WINDY WEATH

OPTIONAL FAIR

W6
W7   W3   W2   W2   W2   W2   W2   W2
W5
W4

3/8" × 3/32" TRAILING EDGE

Copyright by E. KEIL & CO., LTD.,

1. The plan of the Cad

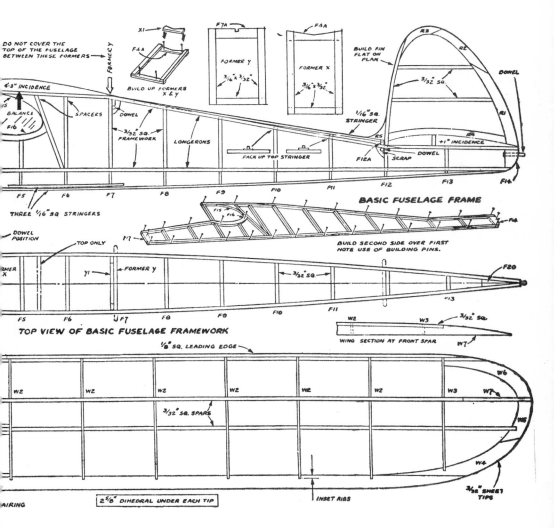

DO NOT COVER THE
TOP OF THE FUSELAGE
BETWEEN THESE FORMERS

FORMER Y

X1

F.4.A

BUILD UP FORMERS
X & Y

F.7.A

FORMER Y

$3/16" \times 3/32"$

F.4.A

FORMER X

$3/16" \times 3/32"$

BUILD FIN
FLAT ON
PLAN

R3

R2

DOWEL

$3/32"$ SQ.

R1

4.3" INCIDENCE

BALANCE

F16

SPACERS

DOWEL

$3/32"$ SQ.
FRAMEWORK

LONGERONS

PACK UP TOP STRINGER

$1/16"$ SQ.
STRINGER

R5

F12A

SCRAP

DOWEL

+1" INCIDENCE

R4

F5

F6

F7

F8

F9

F10

P11

F12

F13

F14

THREE $1/16"$ SQ. STRINGERS

BASIC FUSELAGE FRAME

DOWEL
POSITION

TOP ONLY

F15

F16

F17

BUILD SECOND SIDE OVER FIRST
NOTE USE OF BUILDING PINS.

F4

RMER
X

Y1

FORMER Y

$3/32"$ SQ.

F20

F11

F13

F5

F6

F7

F8

F9

F10

TOP VIEW OF BASIC FUSELAGE FRAMEWORK

W2

W3

$3/32"$ SQ.

WING SECTION AT FRONT SPAR

W7

$1/8"$ SQ. LEADING EDGE

W6

W7

W2

W2

W2

W2

W2

W2

W3

$3/32"$ SQ. SPARS

W5

W4

$3/32"$ SHEET
TIPS

AIRING

$2 5/8"$ DIHEDRAL UNDER EACH TIP

INSET RIBS

1. wingspan glider

CHAPTER 4

Completing the fuselage

Look around you and see what you have made. There are the two fuselage sides, still stuck together as they were when you lifted them from the plan, unless you were particularly painstaking and kept them separate with greaseproof paper. There is the fin, and there is one wing still pinned to the board. In a box close at hand are all the remaining sheet parts cut out, sanded smooth and ready for use. There is also a good deal of mess—if you are like every other aeromodeller before you!

For the sake of good workmanship, your family and your future freedom to build models in peace, the next thing to do is to clear it up. Sweep away all the tiny scraps of wood and the dust, but take care not to throw away any necessary part or usable piece of wood. Put all loose pins back into their tin. With everything orderly again, you are ready to proceed to the next stage.

If the building board is large enough you can now make the tailplane while the first wing is still pinned out. It is made in a very similar manner to the wing. Begin by pinning out the trailing edge and making the notches for the ribs. Then pin out the leading edge, which sits *flat* upon the plan, not like the wing's leading edge which has been inserted corner-wise into "vees" cut in the ribs. Because it is slightly swept back (on the Cadet) pin the leading edge down in two parts, cut at angles on the centre line so that they join neatly. This joint is cemented and a triangular reinforcement piece stuck in place behind. The ribs are then cemented in place, then the tip pieces and finally the single spar. This, too, sweeps back, parallel to the leading edge, so make another angled joint in the middle.

At the centre of the tailplane are two ribs very close together. They should be just wide enough for the base of the fin to fit tightly between them. There is a notch cut in the bottom part of the fin to fit over the tailplane spar. Press the fin into place to check the fit, but do not cement it there yet. Take it out again and lay it to one side if the fit is good. If it is loose, then the two tailplane ribs are a little too far apart.

You can then turn your attention again to the fuselage. The side frames are first separated by running a sharp razor-blade gently between them and slicing through the spots where they are stuck together, at all the cemented joints.

Take the two fuselage formers, X and Y, and from the plan note carefully their positions.

Hold one of the side frames in your hand with the nose pointing upwards and the top towards you. Cement the first former, X, in position on the *left* of the side frame. Hold it there while the cement sets, making sure that it is at a right angle to the side frame—you can test this with a geometry set-square. When the cement has partially hardened, lay the side frame down carefully without dislodging the former. Take up the other side frame and hold it in the same position as the first and cement the second former, Y, in position on the *right* of the frame. Check, too, that this former is at right angles to the side frame.

When the cement has dried thoroughly on both, you can then join the two side frames together by applying cement to the free sides of X and Y and pressing them in their places on the opposite frame. A thin rubber band round each former will hold the two frames together until the cement has dried. Before leaving them to set make sure that the two side frames have been joined together perfectly squarely. At every stage in building the fuselage you must make sure that it is "squared-up", for any inaccuracy will be magnified when the wings and tail are in place and these will not be square to each other. If they are not, then the flying qualities of the model may suffer.

You will already have cut out the other fuselage formers from sheet balsa. Take the nose former and cement this in position, gently bending the forward parts of the two side frames in to meet it, and holding them together with a rubber band until the cement has hardened. The same thing is done with the tail of the fuselage, but this comes to a point and there is no former to be cemented in place. The ends of the frames are slightly bevelled on the insides to make a good joint when they are drawn together. Small triangular pieces are cemented in place at top and bottom and the whole held together with a rubber band until the cement has dried.

On the plan there is a top view of the fuselage structure, showing the **horizontal spacers** which hold the side frames apart. From this drawing you can cut these from strip, in matched pairs, as you did for the vertical spacers. There are one or two spacers which are inserted on the top side only; these are indicated on the plan. When cutting the spacers cut their ends at angles to fit the slope of the side frames, which now curve out from the nose to their broadest point at the cockpit and then taper to a point at the tail. With the spacers cut and matched, cement them in place in line with the vertical spacers to make a rigid "box" framework. Work from the nose to tail and constantly check that the construction is square.

Little remains to be done now to complete the structure of the model. The simplest models have a box fuselage looking very much like yours does at this stage. The designer of the Cadet, however, has improved the look of the model by rounding the fuselage cross section—removing the "boxy" look. There is a little more work to be done on the fuselage, but in appearance it is worth it in the end.

You will have cut from $\frac{1}{16}$ in. sheet a number of small fuselage parts, **sub-formers**, marked with F numbers, and you must now cement these to the horizontal spacers, as marked on the plan, all along the bottom, on the top of the nose back to the windscreen, and immediately in front of the flat platform where the tailplane will be mounted. Slotted into the forward three sub-formers along the bottom of the fuselage is another printed part, the **skid**, which carries the **tow hooks** on which you will attach the tow-line to launch the model. Before cementing the skid in place you must bend the three hooks from the piece of fine wire provided in the kit. This is easily done with a pair of small pliers. Bind these hooks to the skid in the places marked, using fine cotton, and bind them tightly. When you have bound them, coat the bindings liberally with cement and allow time to dry.

Cement the skid in position, and then attach $\frac{1}{16}$ in. square strips into the notches in the sub-formers on the underside, running these strips from nose to tail. These strips, you will notice, are thinner than the longerons and are called **stringers**. Although they add something to the strength of the model, they are primarily there to improve its appearance.

Further stringers are added along the top of the nose, back as far as the windscreen, and one along the fuselage top, from behind the wing mounting to immediately in front of the tail mounting.

Now you can really appreciate the shape of the model. Stick together the noseblock from the pieces cut from the thicker sheet, marked N 1, N 2 and so on, carve and sandpaper this into shape, cementing it very lightly to the front former to do this. When it is shaped, remove it by slicing a razor blade behind it. You will notice that the rear of the noseblock is hollowed out. This is to insert ballast—lead, old cement tube, or plasticine—to weight the nose and make the model balance in the right place.

Cement in place pieces of dowel—the rounded hardwood rod provided in the kit—which serve as pegs for the rubber bands which will hold the wings and tail on. Add the **dashboard**, which slopes downwards from the former in front of the cockpit and cover the space between this former and the dashboard with stiff white paper. You then cement the celluloid windscreen in place. This is already shaped correctly, and needs only to be wrapped round the cabin structure and cemented to the edge of the dashboard and the sheet parts which make the side window frames.

CHAPTER 5

Finishing the structure

The most obvious thing which remains to be done is to join the wings, but we are not quite ready for that yet. The wings have finally to be sanded to the correct aerofoil shape—the leading edge rounded, the trailing edge strip sanded down to a fairly sharp edge and the tips sanded down, too. It is more convenient to do this with the two separate wings than when they are joined together.

Before beginning to sand the leading and trailing edges hold the two wings against each other, flat sides together, and compare the tips—if they are not exact matches then you must make them so by sanding them to shape. Then take one wing panel and hold it with the trailing edge exactly along the front edge of the building board. You can now begin to sand it down to a fine edge. Use a sanding block, and be careful that you do not catch the top edges of the ribs as you move it in long even strokes along the trailing edge. You can save time by removing some of the waste wood with a razor blade, but if you do this, be particularly careful that the razor blade does not "dig" and slice out too much. Do not sand it down to a *very* sharp edge, for it may then splinter. To shape the leading edge simply run the sanding block along the sharp forward corner of the strip, slowly rocking it from top to bottom (taking care not to catch the ribs), and imparting a gentle curve to the front strip. At the tip fine down the leading edge until it meets the tip pieces, and sand these in an outward direction. Keep the bottom side of the tip pieces flat, and sand down the top sides to obtain a fairly fine edge.

Take special care when doing these sanding operations, for a careless slip can spoil a wing, tailplane or fin. These last two, the tail surfaces, are sanded in exactly the same manner, with the slight exception that you sand *both* sides of the fin trailing edge to meet in a fine edge, and not just one side, as you do with wings and tail.

FINISHING THE STRUCTURE

When you have sanded the wings they are ready to be joined. The only cut pieces remaining are some shallow "vee" shaped pieces. These are the **dihedral braces** which are used to reinforce the spars and trailing edge at the centre section when the wings are joined at their shallow vee angle—the **dihedral angle.**

When the wings are in position on the finished model it is intended that each tip should be $2\frac{5}{8}$ in. higher than the centre section. This **dihedral** is best attained by pinning out one wing flat and joining the other to it with twice this distance—$5\frac{1}{4}$ in.—under its tip. You can prop the second wing in position with a pile of books. Cut off first the length of leading and trailing edges and spars on each wing and cut them at an angle, so that you obtain neat joints. Cement the dihedral braces in position to hold the dihedral angle, and finally place the centre rib in position. With one wing flat, this rib must be set at an angle, so that it is upright when the wings are in their correct position. The makers include a small printed part, labelled "W 1 angle template". This is not cemented into the model, but is merely used as a rest for the centre rib when cementing it in position.

An alternative method of building the wings can be seen in the accompanying photos, where the second wing has been built directly on to the first. There is little to choose between the method described and the method illustrated, which you use being purely a matter of preference.

Your work on the wing centre section will probably need some gentle sanding, to remove any roughnesses. Make a thorough check over the whole model to ensure that there are no other roughnesses. If you find any, then sand them smooth. When you have done this, your model is structurally complete. All that remains to be done is to cover it. On the care you take in doing this the performance and certainly the appearance of the model will largely depend.

CHAPTER 6

Covering

Most model aircraft are covered with special kinds of tissue paper, on which is brushed liquid cellulose, called **dope**. This tightens the paper as it dries and makes it impervious to air. Really large models are sometimes covered with fine silk or nylon, while many are covered with both sheet balsa and tissue over certain parts of the structure. Your model, being small and light, however, will be covered with tissue of the finest grade.

Which type of tissue you will choose will depend on the time you wish to spend on covering the model. The type supplied in the kit will need shrinking with water before the dope is applied, but there are tissue papers on sale at most model shops which are as strong and which do not require water-shrinking before doping.

The tissue supplied in your kit, too, is probably all white, and if you wish a your model to be bright you will need to buy coloured tissue. This is preferable to using comparatively heavy coloured dope, for on a small model the weight must be closely watched if performance is not to suffer. With regard to colour it is worth remembering that simple schemes look best and it is advisable to keep the flying surfaces—wings and tail—in light colours. White or yellow wings and tailplane, with red or blue fuselage and fin are suggested. While at the model shop you will need to buy a jar of clear dope, some cellulose "thinners", and a small brush with which to apply it.

With these at hand, you are ready to begin. Cut out a piece of tissue for the fuselage underside, but cut it a little too large all round. With dope, thinned balsa cement, or a paste adhesive such as Dex or Grip-fix stick it to the bottom stringers and bottom longerons, working from the centre stringer outwards, having cut three small slits to slip the paper over the tow-hooks. Ensure that there are no blobs of adhesive under the tissue and be careful to remove all wrinkles. When you have it in place, trim off all excess tissue. The fuselage sides are next covered by attaching the tissue to the longerons, the cockpit window frames and spacers. Again trim off excess paper, using a razor-blade to trim it neatly around the celluloid windows and leaving just enough to turn over the top longerons and to overlap on to the bottom panel. Finally cover the top of the fuselage with two panels; one on the forward fuselage, as far back as the windscreen, and the other between the wing and tail mountings, which are left uncovered. Trim off the excess paper, leaving small overlaps which you stick down along the side panels, remembering that neatness in doing this may not draw attention, but carelessness certainly will. Ragged overlaps are something to be avoided if you want your finished models to be admired.

Covering the wings is done with four panels. Cover the undersides first, with two panels overlapping at the centre, and adhere the paper to the leading and trailing edges, the bottom spar and the tip pieces, and to every alternate rib. Pull out any wrinkles which occur. Wrap the fringe paper over the leading edge and trim off the excess. Wrap about a $\frac{1}{4}$ in. fringe over the trailing edge and trim off the paper around the tip leaving a $\frac{1}{8}$ in. margin. This can then be turned over and stuck to the top surface of the tip by cutting a number of small "vees" in the paper— your mother when making dresses calls them "darts"—closely spaced all round the tip. The top surfaces are then covered in much the same way, with small overlaps folded round to the undersurface. To cover both the fin and tailplane use one panel for each side. When covering the top surface of the tailplane ensure that the paper is firmly stuck to both the centre ribs, for when doped, the strip of paper between them must be cut away for the fin to be inserted.

If the tissue you have used requires water-shrinking there are two ways to do this. One is to spray it with water from a fine scent or insecticide spray but an easier and preferable way is merely to steam it over a boiling kettle until the tissue slackens. Take care on two counts; do not scald your fingers and handle the model gently, for tissue loses much of its strength when wet and it is easy to poke a finger through it. Weight or pin out the flying surfaces while the tissue dries, to prevent warping as the paper shrinks. The lightly-built tailplane is more likely to warp than the wings, but you should guard against distortion in all the flying surfaces.

Do not begin doping until the tissue is thoroughly dry but do not force the drying in front of a fire—it is better to do the water-shrinking in a warm room. The doping *must* be done in a warm atmosphere for when the air is cold and damp, dope "blushes" and dries leaving unsightly white streaks which no further doping will remove. Cellulose is highly inflammable, however, and IT MUST BE KEPT AWAY FROM FLAMES. It also has a strong smell, which some people find unpleasant, so it is advisable to have some ventilation.

Do not attempt to brush on the dope so thickly that it "drags" the tissue, but dilute it with "thinners" so that it flows evenly. Use a soft brush and apply it with smooth, even strokes in a constant direction. Brush across the wings and tailplane rather than along them. Again weight or pin these surfaces to the board to prevent them warping as the dope dries. If you apply the dope thinly it may be advisable to give the model a second coat, but do not do this until the first is thoroughly dry.

When the dope on the tailplane is dry, cut out the strip of paper on the top surface between the two centre ribs and cement the fin in place, ensuring with a set-square that it is perfectly upright.

Attach the wings to the fuselage with thin rubber bands looped over the dowel pegs and across the centre section. The tail unit is attached by looping a band round the rear fuselage and passing it over the tailplane on both sides of the fin and attaching it to the peg at the rear.

Detach the noseblock and place small pieces of lead (cut from an old cement tube) in the cavity. Lightly attach it again and find the **centre of gravity**—the point of balance—of the glider. Add to or reduce the lead ballast until the model balances exactly on the front wing spar and then cement the noseblock firmly in place.

Stand back and survey the result. If it is creditable, congratulate yourself, for your first flying model is complete.

CHAPTER 7

But *how* does it fly?

You will no doubt want to rush straight out to fly the model, but before you fly it you must know how an aeroplane flies. The principles of flight which apply to your 30 in. wingspan, 2 oz. model glider are exactly the same as those which enable the largest jet airliners to fly.

An aircraft in flight must generate an upward force, **lift**, to counteract **gravity**, the downward force which "holds" all people and things to Earth, and which is a result of the Earth spinning rapidly as it orbits the Sun. This lift is generated by the wings.

You will remember from building that the wing has a gently curved upper surface and a flat underside. The effect of this is to cause a difference in speed between the air passing over and under the wings as the aircraft flies through the air. The air passing over the top surface has farther to travel, in passing over the curved top surface, than the air along the flat underside, and it therefore increases in speed, to fill the partial vacuum which would otherwise occur behind the wing. When air is speeded up, its pressure drops and so there is less air pressure acting on the top surface of the wing than there is on the underside, where there is the relatively slower moving air. The high pressure underneath, tending to lift the wing into the region of low pressure above, is the "lifting" force which counteracts the effect of gravity.

Study your model from the side and you will see that the leading edge is raised slightly above the trailing edge. This tilt is the **angle of incidence**, and in the Cadet it is 3 degrees. The effect of the angle of incidence is to improve the lifting qualities of the wing, for the wing's tilt relative to the airflow means that the airflow is compressed against the underside, and increases the lifting force. The greater the angle at which the wing "attacks" the airflow, the greater will be the lift. This applies only *up to a certain angle*, beyond which air resistance, or **drag**, in-

35

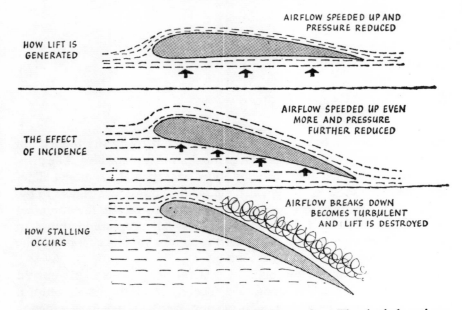

HOW LIFT IS
GENERATED

AIRFLOW SPEEDED UP AND
PRESSURE REDUCED

THE EFFECT
OF INCIDENCE

AIRFLOW SPEEDED UP EVEN
MORE AND PRESSURE
FURTHER REDUCED

HOW STALLING
OCCURS

AIRFLOW BREAKS DOWN
BECOMES TURBULENT
AND LIFT IS DESTROYED

2. How lift is generated by an aerofoil—or flying surface. The shaded sections
represent the wing or tailplane's cross section

creases greatly, flying speed is lost and the smooth airflow over the top
surface of the wing breaks down and becomes turbulent and so destroys the lift. This angle is known as the **stalling angle**.

The wing alone, however, would rotate in the airstream as the air
impinges on its underside, and so it must be stabilized; that is, held so
that it is kept at an efficient **angle of attack**. This is the task of the tailplane. The tailplane is, of course, placed at the end of the fuselage, and
the fuselage acts as a crowbar, or **moment arm**, in magnifying its effect.
The pivot of this crowbar is the **centre of pressure**, which for our purpose can be considered to be at the centre of gravity.

The aircraft is stabilized and prevented from pitching by the airflow
over the tailplane, but another force is needed to hold the aircraft on a
steady course and prevent the nose swinging from side to side. To
contribute this is the purpose of the fin, which also has the fuselage
moment arm through which to act. Any tendency of the nose to swing

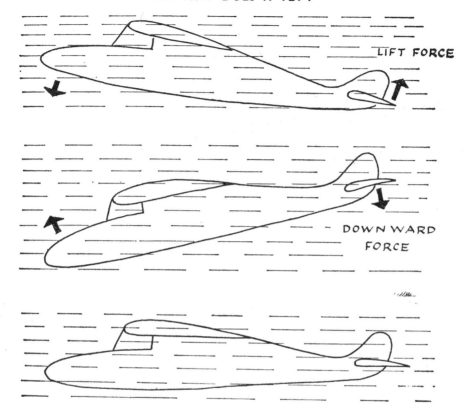

LIFT FORCE

DOWNWARD
FORCE

THE STABILISING EFFECT OF THE TAILPLANE

3. The tailplane, acting through the fuselage "crow-bar", stabilizes the wing and holds it at an efficient angle-of-attack, in the manner shown here

to the left is met by a force acting on the right of the fin, which "pivots" the aircraft, at the centre of gravity, back on course.

There is one other feature of your model which plays a stabilizing part, and that is the **dihedral**, the gentle upward slope of the wings from centre to tips. The dihedral stabilizes the aircraft in the **banking** plane. When one wing drops, its angle of attack and therefore its lift increases and the aircraft is restored to an even keel.

LIFT ON BOTH WINGS EQUAL

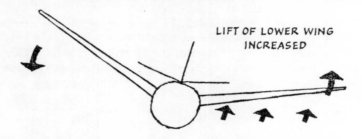

LIFT OF LOWER WING
INCREASED

4. Dihedral—the shallow "V" of the wings—prevents excessive side-slipping and stabilizes the model in the spanwise plane . . . .

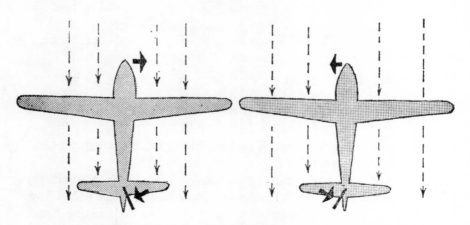

5. . . . while the rudder works exactly as does the rudder of a boat

But how does an unpowered glider move through the air, so that there is air flowing over the wings to generate the vital lift? The answer to this question is—*gravity*.

This downward force, which we are so concerned with counteracting by generating lift, is, in fact, its motive power. Gravity is never completely counteracted in gliding flight, for the aircraft is always sinking along a gentle forward slope. It is always sinking *through the surrounding air*, but air is rarely completely still, and there are often columns of rising air, called **thermals**. If the upward speed of the rising air is greater than the natural sinking speed of the glider through it, then the aircraft will gain height, although it is still sinking through the air. But just as there are rising columns of air, there are also downward currents, and in these the sinking speed of the air will add to the natural sink of the glider. If your model gets in one of these downdraughts, you will see it descend faster than you have come to expect from other flights.

Only the application of power to a model or a full-size aircraft enables it to fly on a level path through the surrounding air, and prevent its gradual descent to the earth. Aircraft engines propel the aircraft through the air, for lift to be generated, by thrusting rearwards a column of air by means of a propeller or in the form of a heated jet. As you progress with aeromodelling, you will build models with their own power.

But first there is your glider to fly and you have the consolation of knowing that there is nothing more graceful than the gentle, silent, floating flight of an unpowered aircraft. All gliders, whether models or man-carrying, have a fascination for their flyers which other aircraft do not possess.

CHAPTER 8

"Trimming" for flight

Before your model is flown off a tow-line, it must be "trimmed" in short flights, launched by hand from shoulder height. Proceed cautiously with trimming flights, just as makers of full-size aeroplanes proceed in small steps with their testing. Before making a complete flight with a new type of aircraft a test pilot lifts it two or three feet off the runway while making a fast "taxi-run" and almost immediately touches-down again. You must prepare your model for tow-line flying in a similarly cautious, step-by-step way.

Wait until the air is absolutely still, or there is the very lightest breeze, before you make your trimming flights. Still-air conditions are often found very early in the mornings or just before dark, but very rarely in the middle of the day. It is best to test glide the model over long grass if possible as this will prevent damage if it descends too rapidly. A clear space twenty or thirty yards long will be enough for trimming flights.

When the right conditions have arrived, assemble your model, and check that you have the wings and tail free from warps and mounted square to each other and to the fuselage. Check once again that the model balances correctly—at the front spar.

If there is any breeze at all, face into it and launch the model gently forwards from the shoulder, with the nose pointing slightly downwards and with the wings level. The glider will do one of several things.

If it flies steadily forwards, sinking gently and landing several yards ahead, you are lucky, for it has no built-in vices and will need very little trimming.

But it may dive sharply to the ground and land almost at your feet. Remembering what you have read in the previous chapter you can work out what must be done. You must increase the angle of attack, so that more lift is generated and the aircraft's rate of descent reduced. But do

40

not alter the angle of attack of the wing simply by inserting packing underneath the leading edge, for this will make the wing mounting unsteady.

All trimming adjustments are made at the tail and to correct a dive you must put packing under the trailing edge of the tailplane. This has the effect of generating a slight downward force at the tail. The aircraft pivots at the centre of gravity, the nose is raised and the wing's angle of attack is increased.

For packing use thin slivers of balsa sheet. Slice $\frac{1}{16}$ in. sheet in two, for adjustments to be made about $\frac{1}{32}$ in. at a time (or buy $\frac{1}{32}$ in. sheet, the thinnest available, at your model shop). Do not make adjustments in greater stages, for they are then likely to be too severe.

Instead of diving, or gliding correctly, your model may stall. It may float on an almost level path, or even climb, immediately it leaves your hand, but after a yard or so it will lose flying speed and then the nose, and probably one wing, will drop suddenly and it will dive towards the ground as it tries to regain flying speed.

The corrective action for a stall is the opposite to that for the dive. You must reduce the angle of attack by packing up the leading edge of the tailplane, to get a slight lifting force at the tail and so lower the nose.

Your model may fly without either stalling or diving but have a tight built-in turn; one wing will drop and the aircraft will move sharply left or right, and possibly hit the ground with one wingtip before the fuselage touches-down. A gentle turn either way is desirable when you are flying the model off the tow-line, for it will reduce the amount of space you will need to fly the model, make it less likely that you will lose it and reduce the distance you have to run each time to retrieve it. But a really tight turn is not wanted, for it will make it difficult to tow the glider to height and there is the danger of a wing breaking if the model lands on it. Therefore trim out a tight turn by slightly off-setting the tail unit so that the fin gives an opposing turning force; if you have a tight turn to the left, move the fin by trailing edge a fraction over to the right, and vice versa. By setting the fin at a slight angle to the aircraft centre line a higher pressure is generated on the forward side than on the rearward side, the whole tail is forced to one side, the aircraft pivots at the centre of gravity, and the nose moves in the opposite direction. If your model glides absolutely straight in its trimming flights then trim in a gentle turn.

When correctly trimmed the model will glide gently to the ground from shoulder height with just a suggestion of a turn. Cement the packing firmly into place. With assistance from one other person, you are then ready for tow-line flights.

You will need a much larger unobstructed space than you needed for trimming flights; in the country you are sure to be able to use some meadow, if you ask the owner's permission, but if you live in a town, you will have to fly in some local park or common, or perhaps in your school playing field. A word of warning—unrestrained toddlers or lively dogs can cause havoc to a model if they get to it before the owner, so be alert if either of these dangers is nearby.

Make your tow-line from a length of strong button thread, *not* ordinary sewing cotton. To one end tie a small curtain ring or a paper clip and a few inches away tie a small piece of rag. Have the thread wound on its reel or any other small piece of wood which is easily held.

For the first flight, attach the tow-line to the front hook. Your helper must hold the model while you unwind about 100 feet of thread and stand *upwind* of him. Together, you both run *into* wind, he with the model held with the noise pointing upwards. As he feels the wings begin to lift, he releases the model with the wings level.

You, at the other end of the tow-line, must keep running into wind. Looking back you will see the model rising on the line behind you. Immediately you stop running the tension on the tow-line will slacken, and helped by the tuft of rag tied beneath it, the tow-ring will drop off the hook and the model will be flying free.

You will not obtain the best performance by towing the model on the front hook, for on this hook it does not climb to the best height. It must be used for the first flights, however, and for any flying when there is considerable wind, for the model is very stable when being towed on this hook. When you have experience of towing, and there are average conditions, you can use the centre hook, and when conditions are absolutely calm, the rear one. When towed up by this, the glider will climb steeply to greater heights, but it will be less stable and tend to swing from side to side on the line.

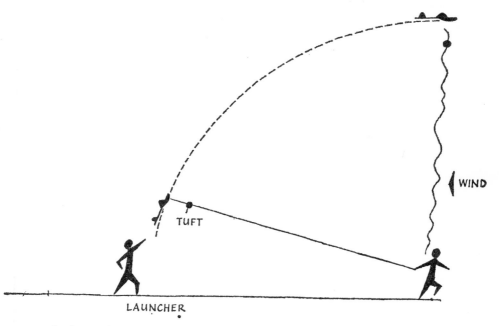

6. A running launch for a model glider—made always *into* the wind

You may want to make a towing winch, which enables you to tow your model to height without much running. For larger, high performance gliders which you may build later, a towing winch is really essential. If you have a small hand-grindstone in your workshop, you can turn it into a winch. Take off the round grindstone and on the spindle mount a tow-line reel made from plywood. A film reel for an 8 mm. film projector, obtainable at a camera shop, may fit your grindstone and serve instead. Make a fine wire guide to project a few inches ahead of the reel to feed the line on to it. Mount the grindstone on a suitable piece of wood, for a handle. Arrange your model, your helper and yourself exactly as you would for a running launch and begin to wind in the line very gently, increasing speed as the model climbs. When you stop winding in, the tow-line will drop free.

In windy conditions, with either running or winch launches, it is sometimes possible to "kite" the model up—after the initial run or winding-in to start it climbing, the model will continue to rise without your running *or* operating the winch. In these conditions, you may have to slacken the line, for it to drop free, by running *towards* the model.

CHAPTER 9

What to build next

Everything written so far in this book has been written to guide you step-by-step in building and flying successfully your first model aeroplane. It is not entertaining reading on its own account and is not meant to be read all at once. If you have kept this book close at hand and consulted it frequently as you have built your first model, and if it has helped you make a creditable model which makes creditable flights, the writer's purpose has been served. The detailed description of building and trimming holds good, with minor variations, for most models you are likely to build in the future.

Building methods for larger gliders, for rubber and engine powered free-flight models, or even for control-line models which give you the thrill of "piloting", will not be substantially different from those you have already followed. You will add to the basic experience and skills acquired as you built your small glider when you build others, but there need be no further detailed step-by-step description of the construction of other models. We shall assume that you have acquired basic knowledge thoroughly.

The question you will be asking is—what comes next? This will depend completely on your inclination and your pocket, but do not be tempted by over-confidence to take too great a step.

If you decide to build another glider, you will have a wide choice of kits at any good model shop, and a larger, higher performance glider or "sailplane" of about 48 in. wingspan should give you no difficulty if you have learned the lessons of the first. Obviously the higher the performance of the model, the more space will be needed in which to fly it. It is well to remind you here *always* to have your name and address or telephone number on any free-flight model, glider or powered, for some day you will have one fly into a thermal, rise and pass out of sight. If your name is on it there will be a good chance that it will be returned.

There are three practical methods of powering model aircraft; by rubber motors, by small internal combustion engines and by cartridges of a slow burning chemical fuel, which generate gases to exhaust through a fine nozzle to give "jet" propulsion.

Of these, rubber power is the oldest, but it has suffered an eclipse in recent years with the advent of tiny diesel engines, very reasonably priced, which can be installed in free-flight models as small as 24 in. wingspan. The solid fuel cartridges, known as Jetex motors, have become popular for certain purposes, particularly for powering realistic scale models of actual jet aircraft.

On cost alone, rubber power, which is the least realistic, wins hands down. Apart from the initial cost of the skein of strip rubber, and the occasional cost of a preservative and lubricating fluid to apply to it, rubber powered models have no running costs. Small diesel engines have small running costs in terms of fuel and their initial costs are naturally well above that of a few yards of strip rubber.

So the kind of power you adopt is as likely to depend on the state of your pocket (or the nearness of Christmas or a birthday) as on any other consideration. You can build an elementary engine-powered free-flight aeroplane as a second model with a good expectation of success, but to build a rubber-powered model is probably the wiser course.

You will find almost as wide a range of kits for these models at any good model shop as there is of glider kits. Select a functional model, which may not look very much like a real aeroplane, but which will perform better than the "scale" rubber-powered models which are also on the market. These miniatures of real aircraft do not fly very well, they are not particularly accurate scale models and the large, slowly rotating fan-like **propeller** needed with a twisted rubber motor destroys what little scale realism they have. If you build a functional model, however, you will have the enjoyment of good performance.

CHAPTER 10

Putting in power

Construction of your first powered model will not differ very much from that of the glider you have built. Work slowly and carefully and make sure that you understand every step, for mistakes are easier to avoid than to correct. Study the plan closely before you begin and have a clear idea of the sequence in which you are going to work.

The only notable structural differences between a simple glider and a simple rubber-powered model aircraft are the provision of an under-carriage, on which the wheels are mounted, and, of course, the installa-tion of a propeller and the means of driving it.

The undercarriage is simply a length of fine spring steel wire (known as piano wire) provided in the kit, which is bent to the appropriate shape with pliers. Make sure that the two axle stubs on which the wheels will be mounted are in line with one another, when seen both from above and from the front. The undercarriage frame is bound to the fuselage structure with button thread, wound closely, and the whole binding is coated liberally with cement.

Suitable wheels can be *laminated* from sheet balsa. This means that each wheel is made up of two or three balsa discs, which are cemented together with the grain of one disc at right angles to the grain of its neighbour. Through the centre of each wheel is driven a short length of fine brass tubing, known as a **bush**, which slides over the axle stub and ensures that the wheel turns smoothly. Ready-made, lightweight plastic wheels, already bushed, can be bought at most model shops and you may prefer to use a pair of these.

The wheels are retained on the axles by soldering a small cup-washer, or a binding of fuse wire, to the end of each axle. This is another skill you are acquiring, and one which will be much needed when you build more advanced models. There is nothing difficult about soldering.

The main points to remember are to ensure that the surfaces you are soldering are absolutely clean and to keep the soldering iron really hot. Take care, too, to "tin" the end of the wire before you put the washer, or fuse wire binding, in place. Leave the axle stubs overlong when you first bend the undercarriage to shape, so that you have enough length on which to work, and cut off the excess when the wheels are in place. You can protect the wheels from being scorched (or melted in the case of plastic wheels) by the heat of the soldering iron, with a wet piece of balsa scrap. Place this over the axle between the wheel and the retaining washer or fuse wire, and break it off when the solder joint is made.

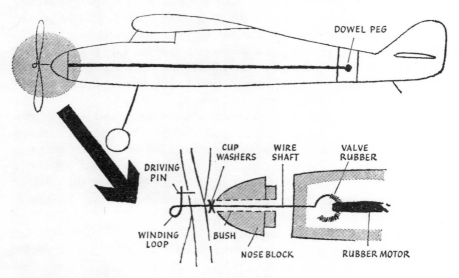

7. A typical rubber-powered model, with the nose details enlarged

Slightly more intricate engineering is involved in the making of the propeller and noseblock assembly. The propeller, which is roughly shaped in most kits, requires careful carving and sanding to shape and its centre must be drilled for a tubular brass bush—in some kits this may already be done. A bush must also be placed through the noseblock, which can either be shaped from block balsa or laminated from pieces of sheet.

Unlike the glider noseblock, this one will not be rigidly attached to the model, for it is drawn forwards when the motor is stretched out and wound. Tension in the rubber motor keeps it in place. At the back of the noseblock is a piece cemented on, which is smaller all round than its neighbour, and which is a firm but removable fit in the open nose of the fuselage.

When drilling both the noseblock and the propeller to insert the bushes you must hold the drill absolutely upright to ensure that the bushes are "true" when inserted. One should have an assistant for this operation, who can squat with his eyes level with the *bit* (the cutting piece) of the drill and can tell you if you are not holding the drill vertically. Do not attempt to drill through either the propeller or noseblock in one operation but drill partly through one side, turn the block or "prop" over, drill through the other side, and then deepen each hole gradually until they meet. Both are best drilled before they are carved and sanded to final shape. Check that the bit you are using in the drill will not make too large a hole to hold the bush firmly.

Constantly check the propeller for balance as you proceed with its final finishing, by balancing it across a knife-edge at its centre. Insert a length of wire through the bush and check its balance on this shaft. When accurately balanced the propeller should remain in any position in which you put it, and when spun it should stop without running back at all in the opposite direction. Finally finish the propeller, when balanced, by applying a light coating of wax polish, which will give a good surface finish and partially proof it against damp.

The propeller and noseblock are then mounted on a common shaft, bent from the appropriate gauge piano wire, with two tiny cup washers between them to serve as bearings, reducing friction. The drive from the shaft will be transmitted to the propeller by bending the front of the shaft backwards so that it hooks on to the front of the propeller. The skein of strip rubber is attached to a hook bent in the rear end of the shaft, behind the noseblock. This hook should be covered with a short length of cycle valve rubber, to prevent the wire cutting the strip rubber. At the other end of the skein, the rubber is anchored to a removable dowel rod peg which slides through a hole on either side of the rear fuselage.

49

The amount and type of rubber for your motor will be specified in the instructions in the kit. It is likely to be $\frac{1}{8}$ in. wide flat strip, which can be bought at most model dealers by the yard, if it is not included in the kit. The specified length of rubber is made up into one large loop, the ends being reef-knotted together.

Before the rubber is installed in the model, wash it in lukewarm soapy water, dry it with a cloth and apply to it the special rubber lubricant, sold at most model shops. Pour a little of the lubricant into the palm of one hand and run the rubber skein through it. Rub the lubricant well into the rubber, and do not leave any excess on it, for any drops which fall on to the model structure will probably rot the balsa and certainly spoil the appearance of the tissue.

When it is lubricated the rubber is ready to be hooked between the prop-shaft and the rear fuselage peg. Make up the skein into the appropriate number of strands over your helper's wrists, making sure that the tension is exactly the same in each strand. One end of the skein can then be attached to the prop-shaft and the motor lowered into the fuselage, which is held vertically. The rear fuselage peg is then inserted. You must ensure that you have all the strands of rubber passing round this peg.

The number of turns which a rubber motor can take without breaking varies enormously according to the quality of the rubber, its thickness, length of the skein and so on. There will be an approximate number given in the instruction leaflet for the particular model you have built. Follow this, but do not apply the safe maximum number of turns all at once. A rubber motor, like a car engine, must be "run in", and you should work gradually up to the safe maximum, in several motor runs, increasing the number of turns each time. Remember, too, that a motor will take more turns safely if it is wound slowly than if it is wound rapidly, for uneven stresses in the rubber are then less likely to occur.

Never be tempted to exceed the safe number of turns, to achieve longer flights, for you will then risk breaking the rubber. When this happens, it can tear a fuselage to pieces in a flash and will certainly damage it considerably. You must also remember that a rubber motor in tension is exerting considerable stresses on the fuselage structure, tending at once to telescope it and to twist it. An over-tensioned motor can, therefore, damage or smash a model without itself breaking.

To avoid these disasters you must develop a strict routine. Before the start of every flying session lubricate the motor and carefully inspect it for any signs of weakening. If you get any dirt, sand or grit on the rubber do not use it until you have washed and dried it thoroughly and re-lubricated. Wash off old lubricant if the motor is not going to be used for some weeks and store the rubber in a closed, clean tin or box. Never leave a rubber motor in a model for longer, say, than a week-end, for light has a deteriorating effect on it.

The final point to remember in the correct treatment of your rubber motor is never to leave it long in tension. Once the motor has been wound the model should be released as soon as possible, or the motor allowed to unwind if for some reason you cannot fly.

You can wind the motor simply by turning the propeller backwards (clockwise, when seen from the front) with a finger. This method is tedious and if one has a long and successful flying session, with many flights, it will probably give you a stiff wrist. Its only advantage is that you can fly the model single-handed—if you have a helper available then there is a much better way.

This is the use of an ordinary hand-drill as a winder, with a thick wire hook, or the looped end of a meat skewer, firmly gripped in its *chuck*. The winder hook is engaged with the loop in the front of the prop-shaft and the propeller and noseblock drawn out from the fuselage.

Your helper holds the model with one hand around the nose and one around the fuselage forward of the tailplane, and he must take care not to dislodge the rear fuselage peg. You stand a yard or so back, so stretching the motor—but not too much, for remember the stresses on the fuselage structure. You then wind the hand-drill, counting how many times you turn its handle.

Most hand-drills are geared in the ratio of about 3 to 1, which means that for every one turn of the drill handle, three will be put in the motor. Before using the winder, therefore, check how it is geared and work out the number of turns you must make with the winder for the required number in the motor.

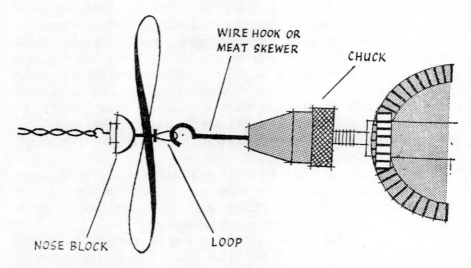

8. An ordinary hand-drill makes an ideal winder and a shortened meat skewer the ideal winding hook. Check that the hook is firmly clamped in the drill's chuck

As you wind and the tension on the motor increases, walk gradually towards the model. Your helper stands still. When the motor is fully wound the noseblock is slipped into place, and the propeller is held until a fraction of a second before the model is launched.

CHAPTER II

Flying rubber-powered models

N ow that you have a model with power installed, you will be intro-
duced to new forces acting on the model in flight. There are, of
course, our old friends **gravity**, or weight, which is opposed by **lift**, and
drag, the resistance of the air as the model moves through it, which tends
to hold the model back. But whereas drag was counteracted in the glider
by the forward motion as the model sank through the surrounding air
under the effect of gravity, you now have **thrust**. This is a positive, forward push generated by the propeller as it "bites" against the air and
throws it rearwards.

The model, therefore, is no longer committed always to sinking
through the air to gain its forward motion, for as long as there is sufficient thrust to overcome the drag, the aircraft will accelerate. The lift
will increase and if it overcomes the weight the model will rise. When
the power is spent, drag takes over, and the aircraft loses speed, lift
decreases and the aircraft sinks in a forward glide.

But there is one other force, an odd one, called **torque**. This is a reac-
tion to the power turning the propeller anti-clockwise and it is tending to
turn the whole model in the opposite, clockwise, direction; that is, the
left wing is tending to drop, and the model is tending to turn to the left.
Obviously torque, which is met in rubber- and engine-powered models,
but not in gliders or Jetex-powered ones, is only encountered during the
powered phase of the flight, and ceases when the motor stops. It must,
nevertheless, be allowed for in trimming for flight.

Initial trimming is the same as that for gliders. Weight the model so
that it balances level at the indicated point—about one-third back along
the width of the wing, or $33\frac{1}{3}$ per cent **chord**. Check that it is completely
free from warps. Choose a calm day and face into what little wind there

is. Launch the model on a gentle downward slope from shoulder height, preferably over long grass. Have the propeller in the horizontal position to reduce the chance of its breaking if the model dives into the ground. Make the trimming adjustments you have already learned; packing under the tailplane trailing edge to correct a dive and under its leading edge to correct a stall. Aim for a gentle, smooth glide to the ground.

We know that without any adjustment, torque will cause the model to turn to the left under power. Do not, therefore, trim in a gliding turn to the left, for this added to the left turning tendency under power may produce too sharp a turn and make the model spin into the ground. Trim in a gentle gliding turn to right. More right turn is needed in the powered phase, to counteract torque, than will be needed in the gliding phase. This additional right turning tendency is obtained by side-thrust—deflecting the propeller a little to the right. This is done by inserting a thin sliver of balsa behind the *left* side of the noseblock. Balsa packing behind the noseblock can have quite drastic effects, so make adjustments very gradually, with the thinnest slivers of wood, which are cemented in place when the best adjustment is reached.

The motor can be hand wound for its first flight with only about a third of the recommended number of turns. Launch the model slightly nose-high into wind with a gentle push.

If your model tends to stall in power flight, but is perfectly satisfactory in the glide, a further thrust adjustment is needed. This is **down-thrust**, obtained by putting balsa packing behind the *top* of the noseblock. The effect of this is to prevent the model assuming such a nose-high climbing attitude that the angle of attack of the wings passes stalling point, the airflow over them breaks down and lift is lost.

Gradually apply more turns to the motor, making any thrust adjustments which appear necessary. When well trimmed, your model will climb steeply from your hand, turning gently to the right. The climb will become less steep as the motor runs down, the model will then level out and eventually enter the glide, still turning to the right.

When you have the model flying well you can make it perform proper take-offs, or r-o-g (rise-off-ground) flights as they are known to experienced aeromodellers. Do not try an r-o-g flight if the model shows any tendency to a *tight* turn under power, if both wheels do not run freely and if there is no really smooth surface available. A large piece of plywood, or the top of your model box, if you have acquired one, will make a suitable "runway". As with hand launching, the model must be pointed into wind.

CHAPTER 12

Why not a jet?

In 1948, when jet aircraft were still quite a novelty and not the most common occupants of the skies, as they are today, two English engineers greatly excited the model aircraft world. They marketed small, very light jet propulsion motors, known as Jetex units, which have since become popular with aeromodellers the world over.

A Jetex unit is not an engine in the normal sense, having no moving parts, but is a light alloy cylinder into which pellets of a specially made slow-burning, non-explosive solid fuel are inserted. The cylinder is closed by an end cap, in the centre of which is a fine jet nozzle. This is attached by a spring-loaded clip, in the smallest units, and by two clips in the case of the larger motors. When the fuel pellet burns, having been ignited by a plastic fuse, high-pressure gases build up in the cartridge and are expelled at speed through the nozzle, producing thrust. If the nozzle becomes clogged, the spring retainers of the end cap expand, permitting the escape of the gases around its rim and so preventing the cartridge bursting through excessive pressure.

Having no moving parts, Jetex motors have almost endless lives, providing that they are kept clean. The fuel leaves considerable carbon deposits when it burns and it is essential that these are scraped away from the interior of the barrel, between every second or third flight. Special scrapers are provided with every motor. The jet nozzle, too, must be regularly cleaned between flights—a wet pipe cleaner is ideal for this task, with the larger units, and special nozzle cleaners are provided with the really small motors. The asbestos washer which fits inside the end cap becomes charred, and must be replaced regularly. This will prevent gas leakages around the flanges of the cap and consequent losses of thrust.

The deposits have a highly corrosive effect on the light alloys of

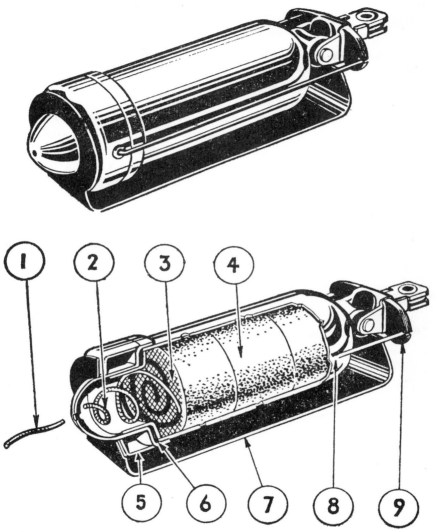

9. A small Jetex solid fuel "jet" motor. The key is as follows: (1) and (2) ignition fuse; (3) gauze disc; (4) fuel pellets; (5) nozzle and cap piece; (6) asbestos sealing washer; (7) mounting clip; (8) cartridge body; (9) closing springs

which the motors are made, and they can quickly render a Jetex useless. It is important, therefore, that the whole unit is thoroughly washed in warm soapy water at the end of each flying session.

If these simple procedures are followed, Jetex-powered model flying can be very enjoyable and quite inexpensive. The units slide easily into spring clips permanently attached to the model, and are removed for reloading. The smallest motors take one pellet and have, therefore, a fixed running time. The larger ones hold one, two or three charges and their burning times can thus be varied, according to the amount of space available in which the model is to be flown.

The case with which the fuel pellet slides into the cartridge provides an indication of carbon deposits; if it is difficult to insert the charge, the cartridge needs to be scraped out. With the pellet in place a length of fuse is coiled twice or three times and pressed firmly against the face of the fuel pellet and a gauze disc pressed down on top of it, to hold it against the charge. The gauze also acts as a filter, preventing small pieces of solid matter reaching and clogging the nozzle. One end of the fuse is led over the edge of the gauze disc, and touches another short length of fuse poked through the jet nozzle and protruding about a quarter of an inch from it. The Jetex is then ready for sliding or screwing into its mounting bracket. The model is held in the launching position, the fuse ignited, and immediately the hiss of the escaping jet is heard, it is launched.

Fuses can be ignited with matches, but it is obvious that you must be careful when plying a naked flame near your model not to set light to anything else. If you have an adult helper who smokes, his cigarette will be ideal for lighting the fuse. Care in loading will be repaid by an absence of false starts, when the fuse burns out without igniting the fuel. If this happens it means that the fuse has not been pressed tightly against the face of the fuel charge, or that the coils into which it is wound are touching each other. The coiled fuse should be spread well over the face of the fuel charge, to obtain even ignition over its whole surface and thus the maximum thrust.

The five Jetex units available weigh between $\frac{1}{4}$ oz., when loaded, for the smallest, the Atom 35, and $1\frac{9}{16}$oz. for the largest, the Scorpion, and they deliver thrusts ranging from $\frac{1}{2}$ oz. (Atom 35) to 4 oz. (Scorpion).

58

All but the Atom 35 are available with **augmenter tubes**. These are variable lengths of aluminium jet pipes with one belled end, into which the motor is pointed. The jet of gases expelled from the motor entrains additional air from around the motor into the bell-shaped intake and sucks this through the tube. In this way the total thrust is increased. In the case of the Scorpion, a motor designed particularly for contest flying, the augmenter tube increases thrust from about 4 oz. to over 5 oz.

Augmenter tubes have another advantage. They are in effect miniature versions of the long jet pipes which are necessary in most modern jet fighter aircraft, where the engine, for weight considerations, must be mounted amidships at about the centre of gravity. These tubes make possible scale models of many modern jet aircraft, with the Jetex motor, too, mounted in the "scale" position. When used in this way, the augmenter tube can comprise the main structural part of the fuselage, which is in effect built around it. It is necessary, however, to use special long ignition strips to light the fuse of a "buried" engine.

The Jetex makers market a large range of kits for scale models of modern jet fighters, which use the augmenter tube method. In this range are flying models of such aircraft as the Hawker Hunter, the Folland Gnat and the Lockheed Starfighter. These models, which are all around 9 in. span, fly fast and realistically. All are powered by the $\frac{5}{16}$ oz. Jetex 50C, which delivers 5 oz. thrust with its augmenter tube. The kits are to a large extent pre-fabricated, and assembly of these models takes little time. Several other manufacturers market kits designed for Jetex power. From simple solid balsa "chuck" gliders, on which the Atom 35 can be installed, to large but lightweight endurance models for contest flying, there are many models suitable for this form of power.

The absence of any rotary motion means that there is no torque to affect the model in flight, as there is in propeller-driven models. Trimming them for turning flight is therefore simply a matter of rudder deflection, left or right. Trim first to obtain a gentle glide. If the model climbs too steeply under power and stalls, down thrust must then be applied. This is done by inserting packing under the front end of the mounting bracket, if the motor is mounted on top of the model, and at the rear end if it is mounted on the underside. If it does not climb steeply enough, then a little upthrust is needed and packing must go at the rear of the bracket for a top-mounted motor and at the front for one mounted underneath. These adjustments must be made in very small degrees.

Jetex motors themselves are virtually indestructible in the course of model flying, but in those models where they are mounted underneath the mounting bracket itself may be displaced in the landing. For those models where the motor is mounted externally, the best position is certainly on top, rather than beneath, to overcome this danger. If you build a model with a Jetex motor mounted underneath, therefore, make a point after every landing to check that the mounting bracket has not been moved. Even comparatively small displacements of the thrust line can have unexpected, and unwelcome, effects in flight.

CHAPTER 13

About engines

After you have been aeromodelling a short time, you are likely to want a model aero-engine as a power plant. There are three kinds of internal combustion engine developed for use in model aircraft—petrol (or spark ignition) engines, diesel (or compression ignition) engines and glow plug (or hot coil) engines. Of these the petrol engine is the oldest, but it is now the most rarely used.

All the early model aircraft power plants were petrol engines (except for a few compressed air motors). They were big and heavy, with their need for batteries, coil and a contact mechanism to produce the carefully timed spark with which the petrol vapour inside the engine's cylinder was ignited. It was not until the modern diesel engine was developed in Switzerland about seventeen years ago that there came about practical power plants for small model aeroplanes, suited for operation by far-from-expert and far-from-wealthy aeromodellers.

The diesel engine needs no spark to ignite the explosive vapour drawn into the cylinder, and thus it dispenses with any electrical accessories. The fuel vapour is ignited by the heat which is generated when the fuel-air mixture is compressed within the cylinder. (If you need proof that the temperature of air rises when it is compressed, make a few vigorous strokes on a cycle pump with one finger over the nozzle. You will find both your finger and the pump barrel will become quite warm.)

The light and simple diesel engine spread rapidly to Britain and most aeromodelling countries of the world, and has now been highly developed. There is now a wide range of engines available, including both general purpose "sport" engines and very high performance engines for contest flying. The greatest benefit of the diesel engine was that it made possible inexpensive power models as small, or smaller, than your first glider. "Thimble sized" engines, for the smallest model aeroplanes, are now on sale for as little as £1 15s.

The glow plug engine is something of a hybrid which first became popular in the U.S.A. This kind of engine has a special plug in the cylinder head, through which a current, from a dry battery or accumulator, is passed for starting. Once the engine is running the battery is disconnected and the high temperatures generated by ignition of the special fuel keep the plug glowing to ignite the subsequent intake of explosive vapour. The "electrics", though needed on the ground are, therefore, not needed in the model. Very small glow plug motors are now marketed here, although there is not such a wide choice as there is of diesels.

The cheapness, simplicity and reliability of the small diesel engine together with its docility, make it the obvious and ideal choice for your first power unit, before you progress to larger and "hotter" diesels, or to more complex motors of another type.

Before buying and operating an engine it is worthwhile to have a basic knowledge of how it will function. On the facing page is an "exploded" drawing of a modern diesel, the 1·5 c.c. E.D. Super Fury. "1·5 c.c." is a measure of its cylinder capacity, in cubic centimetres, which in turn is an approximate guide to its power. Cubic centimeters is the British and European method of classifying engines—the capacity of American-made ones on the British market is measured in cubic inches, or rather, fractions of cubic inches.

Imagine the parts seen in the exploded drawing all fitted together, with a **fuel pipe** connected to the near end of the **jet**. As the engine is turned by hand, by means of the propeller mounted on the front of the **crankshaft**, between the **driver** and the **nut**, the **piston** will rise and fall in the **cylinder**. As it rises, it will cause a partial vacuum, or low pressure region, in the **crankcase**. In this phase the missing segment of the **rotary disc**, which is driven by the pin on the back of the crankshaft, will be opposite the **venturi** opening in the **backplate**. Thus air will be sucked into the crankcase through the venturi and will pass around the jet, drawing fuel through the small hole in the side of the jet and vapourizing it. The amount of fuel sucked in is controlled by the tapered **needle** and **thimble**, which can be screwed in and out to partially block the jet from

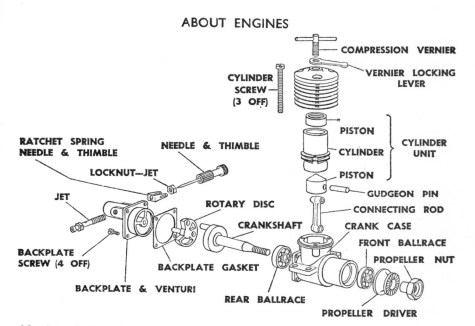

COMPRESSION VERNIER

VERNIER LOCKING LEVER

CYLINDER SCREW (3 OFF)

PISTON

CYLINDER UNIT

RATCHET SPRING NEEDLE & THIMBLE

NEEDLE & THIMBLE

CYLINDER

LOCKNUT—JET

PISTON

JET

GUDGEON PIN

ROTARY DISC

CONNECTING ROD

CRANKSHAFT

CRANK CASE

FRONT BALLRACE

BACKPLATE SCREW (4 OFF)

PROPELLER NUT

BACKPLATE GASKET

BACKPLATE & VENTURI

REAR BALLRACE

PROPELLER DRIVER

10. A typical modern model diesel engine is shown "exploded" in this drawing. The workings are explained on adjacent pages. This particular engine is the E.D. Super Fury, a high performance 1·5 c.c. engine with an outstanding reputation. It is, perhaps, a little "hot" for a first engine, but it has some ideal smaller brothers

the fuel pipe. An explosive mixture of air and fuel vapour will be drawn into the crankcase.

Imagine now the piston travelling on the downward stroke. It will compress the mixture in the crankcase, which cannot escape backwards through the venturi, as this has now been sealed by the rotary disc. Its only escape is upwards, through the **transfer ports**—vertical grooves in the walls of the crankcase and cylinder, which deliver the mixture into the cylinder, above the piston. The piston then begins to rise again as it passes *bottom dead centre* and the **connecting rod**, which drives the crankshaft through the same pin which links the crankshaft and the rotary disc, passes the vertical. The piston rises in the cylinder, compressing the air-fuel mixture. The temperature rises and at the top of the stroke, *top dead centre*, the engine fires. The mixture explodes and expands, driving the piston down again. As the piston travels downwards,

63

it will clear the **exhaust ports**, which are horizontal slots in the cylinder walls between the two fins seen on the cylinder in the drawing. The expanding gases will escape through these exhaust ports, while the new charge of air-fuel mixture, drawn into the crankcase on the previous upstroke, is compressed in the crankcase and driven into the cylinder through the transfer ports. The two strokes of the piston have given one complete revolution of the crankshaft. The whole cycle is then repeated—but in an incredibly shorter time than it has taken to read about it. Most model diesel engines operate at rotary speeds of between 10,000 and 15,000 revolutions a minute.

The **compression ratio** of the engine, on which will depend the rise in temperature of the air compressed within the cylinder, can be varied by the **contra piston**, which is at the top of the cylinder. This can be pushed down by means of the **compression vernier**, which is screwed through the **cylinder head**, which has several **fins** to increase its surface area and enable more engine heat to be carried away by air passing around it.

When the contra piston is forced down the cylinder by the vernier, the compression ratio rises, and the engine becomes harder to turn over. When it is slackened off compression will drive the contra piston up the cylinder, to bear against the vernier again, and thus compression will be reduced. In many engines the contra piston is very stiff, and will sometimes only be driven up when the engine fires. The ability to increase or decrease compression and the amount of fuel sucked in once the engine is running does much to contribute to the smooth running and ease of handling of the small diesel engine.

The adjustable compression enables the use of many different propellers, each of which causes the engine to run at different speeds, and allows the firing of the fuel to be re-timed once the engine has warmed up, when the heat of the cylinder would tend to fire the engine too early on each stroke. This is compensated for simply by reducing compression once the engine has started.

When buying your first engine, be very suspicious about any second-hand ones offered. If one is offered by a reputable dealer who has tested it, it will probably be satisfactory, but a private offer may not be so. The engines on the market now are so reasonable in price that there is little to be gained by buying a used one.

64

CHAPTER 14

Running your first diesel

Almost any diesel between 0·5 c.c. and 1·5 c.c. will be eminently suitable for your first engine. Generally speaking the larger the engine the more expensive it will be and, of course, the models to accommodate it will cost more to build. Engines in this range are numerous. Thousands of aeromodellers have flown their first power models with the E.D. Bee, a 1 c.c. engine which has an immense reputation. Its younger, and smaller, brother is the E.D. Pep, an 0·8 c.c. motor. The smaller Mills 0·75 c.c. is another well-established favourite. Two engines particularly suitable for newcomers to power flying are the Frog 80 of 0·8 c.c. and the Frog 100 of 1 c.c. The E.D. Super Fury, the engine seen in the exploded diagram, has a reputation for outstanding performance in the 1·5 c.c. range—its power is probably as much as you would want to handle in your first engine. Allen Mercury market two high performance diesels of 1·0 c.c. and 1·5 c.c. respectively. Another 1·0 c.c. motor which is regarded highly is the M.E. Heron.

This list is by no means exhaustive—there are many others you can consider.

The first thing to do after purchase is to read thoroughly the makers' instructions—and to resist any temptation to take the engine to pieces for dismantling will probably cancel any gurantee and will certainly damage the seals made between the various parts. With some engines a suitable propeller will be supplied, but with most this will be an additional item to buy. The diameter and pitch measurements of suitable propellers will vary according to the kind of model you intend the motor for. For free-flight models the **pitch**—the theoretical distance that the propeller tends to screw itself through the air with one revolution—is fine and with control line models it is coarser. Thus an engine which turns a 9-in.

propeller with **4** in. pitch for free flight will probably use an 8 in. diameter by 8 in. pitch (8 × 8) propeller for control line flying.

The engine must be mounted firmly on a block or two bearers
screwed to a bench or table. Do not clamp the engine in a vice—it may
distort it. You can, of course, mount the engine on a block and clamp
the block in the vice—providing the vice is sufficiently heavy to hold the
engine steady. The propeller can then be mounted on the crankshaft, and
its retaining nut tightened. The correct propeller position is for one
blade to be at the "one o'clock" position when seen from the front, as
the piston comes up to top dead centre, and full compression is felt.

Use only a fuel recommended by the makers for the first runs of your
engine. Both ordinary fuels and "doped" high performance mixtures
can be bought ready mixed at any model shop. With variations, diesel
fuels usually consist of a three-part mixture, containing roughly equal
proportions of paraffin, ether (an alchoholic spirit) and a lubricating oil.

A word of warning about fuels. They are highly inflammable and the
ether, whose purpose in the mixture is to lower the temperature at
which it will ignite—its **flash point**—is a mildly dangerous fluid. Dangerous, that is, only if sensible precautions are not taken. Keep any naked
flames away from diesel fuel, and do not put your nose right over it and
breathe its vapour for long periods of time, for ether has an intoxicating
effect, and can even make one unconscious—but only if you make a
point of inhaling it for a long time.

When running an engine indoors, make sure there is plenty of ventilation for the fumes to escape. Handle the fuel carefully, and do not
"slosh" it around. Special filler cans for putting the small quantities of
fuel needed into the tank can be bought at model shops, and it is worth
having one of these. They have the advantage that the spout can be
completely closed when it is not in use, preventing the ether evaporating.
Always remember to keep the tops of fuel containers screwed tightly on
when fuel is not required, to prevent evaporation. A mixture which has
lost a lot of its ether through evaporation will not ignite in the engine,
and you may try for hours to start it, without success and without realiz-
ing the cause.

Make sure, too, that no dirt gets in the fuel. Absolute cleanliness pays
in a longer life—the tiniest pieces of grit in the fuel can soon ruin an

engine and at best, will block the fuel jet and stop the engine—or prevent it even starting. Always use absolutely clean containers for fuel and if you suspect that some fuel is contaminated, then throw it away.

Every engine is test run before it leaves the factory and with it you will receive a card showing the best settings for the compression vernier and the throttle—so do not fiddle with these and lose the maker's settings, otherwise it may take you some time to find them again when trying to start the engine.

The engine, then, is firmly mounted on your workbench and there is no obstruction in the area that the propeller will sweep. The tank is filled with fresh, clean fuel and the controls are at the maker's settings. Fuel is drawn into the engine by placing one finger over the venturi and flicking the propeller over compression two or three times, in an anti-clockwise direction. Remove your finger from the venturi to avoid drawing too much fuel into the engine, or it will become flooded. When this happens, the cylinder above the piston becomes full of fuel and it is difficult to turn the engine over compression. If more than ordinary force seems necessary to turn the engine over, *do not force it*. Liquid is almost incompressible and to attempt to turn the engine over when the cylinder is full of fuel may result in the connecting rod becoming bent. If it is flooded, turn the propeller *clockwise* until the piston is at the bottom of its stroke, and the exhaust ports are open. Blow through them to expel the excess fuel.

Flick the propeller over compression smartly to start the engine, using the right forefinger placed at the root of the blade. A sharp flick should make the engine fire. If there has been no firing after five or six flicks, suck a little more fuel into the engine, by choking with your finger over the venturi. If there is still no firing after a few flicks, but signs that fuel is getting through to the cylinder, raise the compression slightly by turning the vernier through one-quarter of a turn. This should do the trick and then the engine should fire, pick up and run.

When you have the engine running, you can then see for yourself the effect of adjusting the controls. If you close the throttle slightly the engine will pick up speed—in fact most engines require a slightly more open throttle for starting than they require for the best running and it is the usual thing to reduce the amount of fuel in the indrawn air by closing the throttle once the engine is warm. If you go on closing the throttle, however, the engine will become hesitant and then stop. Open it up too much and it will backfire and lose power.

Similarly, you can gingerly turn the compression vernier through a turn or so. Raise the compression too much and the engine will again begin to backfire; lower it too much and the power will die away, although a slight reduction in compression, as with throttle, is usually required once the engine is warm..

But maybe your engine will not simply fire and run smoothly. If it begins by backfiring the compression is probably too high—and you may learn this the hard way by having the propeller give you a stinging "thwack" over the knuckles. Don't be discouraged—you will soon acquire the knack of flicking the propeller and yet keep your fingers out of harm's way. It is possible, too, that the fuel-air mixture is too rich, so close the throttle slightly.

If the engine is difficult to start when cold, you can *prime* it by squirting a little fuel through the open exhaust ports—this is another reason why it is a good thing to have a filler can with a fine nozzle. Do not over prime, however, for it is very easy to flood the cylinder with too much fuel.

For its first runs, do not be tempted to run your engine at its fastest speeds, but adjust it so that it is running at somewhere below its maximum revolutions per minute (known as r.p.m., or simply "revs"). Like any new machinery, big or small, your engine will last longer and perform better if it is gently treated until it is thoroughly "run in". You will, in any case, want to keep stopping and re-starting your engine until you know it thoroughly.

Do not be discouraged if it is not too easy first time. If you keep in mind what you have read here, and read thoroughly the instruction booklet provided with the engine, you will soon know it inside-out. Once you have it well adjusted, keep to those compression and throttle settings, and always use a fuel mixture you know your engine likes. In this, the maker's recommendation is usually the best guide.

CHAPTER 15

Power model flying

You have an engine and you know how to run it, so what about a model? Here again, the choice is immensely wide—your dealer will be able to guide you in your choice. Again, the choice of a simple, rugged sport model is wise for your first "power job"—be warned away from tricky, high performance types until you have gained experience.

The model you choose will probably be about 36 or 40 in. wingspan if your engine is about 0·8 c.c.–1 c.c. Its construction will be no more difficult than those you have already built. You will, however, have to build in hardwood bearers on which the engine is bolted, and you will make a stiffer undercarriage than you have made before. Accuracy in lining up the engine bearers exactly as shown on the plan is very important. Remember too, that model diesel fuel has a pretty harmful effect on a model's structure over a period of time, so heavily dope the **engine bay**, inside and out, to give it the best protection. Never slosh fuel around a model if you want it to last; if you spill any accidentally, or overfill the tank, always wipe away the excess.

Check always that the engine is firmly bolted into the model, remembering that vibration will tend to loosen the nuts on the mounting bolts. Here, too, you are helped by model suppliers, for **lock nuts** are made down to the smallest sizes. These incorporate fibre washers which firmly grip the threads on the bolt, and will not slacken through vibration. Use them in preference to plain nuts.

Proceed with trimming the model for flight just as you have done before, in the same calm conditions and, preferably, over the same shock-absorbing long grass. After checking that the wings and tailplane are squarely mounted, put the propeller in the horizontal position so that a blade will not be broken if the model dives. (With flexible plastic propellers, which are now very common, this precaution is not so important.)

Launch the model in the same gentle nose-down attitude as you have done before but give it a slightly harder push than you did your glider and rubber models, remembering that its flying speed is probably greater. Trim it for a gentle glide to ground using the trimming adjustments you have already learned. When you obtain this glide, you are ready for power-trimming flights:

It is very likely that when building the model, you were advised, on the plan, to build in a little *downthrust*. The effect of downthrust is explained in Chapter 11, on rubber-powered models, and its purpose is precisely the same in the power model. It is to prevent the nose rising too high when the model is under power so that it either loops or stalls. But whereas with the rubber model you slipped a balsa sliver behind the noseblock, in a power model you obtain downthrust by putting very thin washers on the *rear* engine mounting bolts, underneath the mounting lugs, or in the case of a radially mounted engine (not very common in Britain), behind the engine backplate on the *top* bolts only. It is wise to follow any instructions concerning downthrust given on the plans and if none is given, it is still very prudent to mount the engine with slight downthrust at least for the first flights. But remember, any adjustments made by altering the thrust line of the model—that is, by physically displacing the engine—have a considerable effect, so make these adjustments in *very* small degrees.

The length of engine run you can afford to have without risking losing the model will, of course, depend on the amount of space you have in which to fly it, but even with fairly short runs you are obviously going to need larger space than when you flew the Cadet. Before making the first flights remember to put your address on the model. For the first power-trimming flights you should not have more than a run of about 10 seconds. The safest way of ensuring this is to time how long the engine runs on a full tank. If it runs, say, for 1 minute and 45 seconds before stopping, then fill the tanks and allow it to run for 1 minute 35 seconds before launching the model. This is, of course, extravagant with fuel; another way is to know how long the engine will run with, say one or two full squirts from your filler-can and to put in the appropriate number.

A final check then, before flight. Address on model—yes! Engine firmly mounted—yes! Propeller nut tightened fully—yes! Flying surfaces all lined up—yes! Rudder set for a right turn—yes! (This will counteract the leftward torque turn, as explained in Chapter 11, to give a straight power flight and a turn to the right during the glide.) You known the wind direction, in which the model must be launched—yes!

Right—you're ready to go!

Start the engine, adjust it to run at far less than its full power, face into wind, hold the model above your head and wait until there is only a few seconds fuel remaining. Run slowly into wind, keeping the model's nose slightly upward, wings level. Launch it with a s-m-o-o-t-h forward thrust. Study carefully the model's behaviour.

If you have a perfectly trouble-free first flight, run and retrieve the model and as you walk back check that nothing has been displaced on landing. For the subsequent flights you can gradually increase the engine power and the length of run to a sensible limit—say 30 seconds for a reasonably large flying field.

But maybe you are not so lucky. If the model stalls under power, increase downthrust. If it climbs steeply and turns on to its back before diving frighteningly, you definitely need downthrust—but rather more of it! If it turns gently either left or right under power, leave well alone—but remember that as you increase power on subsequent flights, torque and the tendency for the aircraft to turn to the left will increase. If you have a tight power turn to the left which forces the nose down into a dive, increase right rudder, but not to the extent of forcing a right spiral dive on the glide.

If the model still turns sharply with torque, check that there is no unintentional left *sidethrust* aiding the natural tendency of the model to turn to the left. A little right sidethrust may be needed to counteract torque but generally this should be very slight. It is not usual to require any sidethrust, however, in models which are not excessively powered—and if you have chosen your first power model wisely, you will not have built a tricky model with a very high power:weight ratio. Normally, rudder adjustments will serve to trim the model for both powered and gliding phases; a certain degree of right rudder producing a gentle turn under power and a tighter turn in the glide.

Increase power in easy stages in the early flights, for slight trim changes are likely as power (and torque) is increased. But doing this in a gradual way you can detect the changes and make trimming allowances for them but obviously a sudden jump from half power, and thus low propeller thrust, to full revs and high thrust may produce equally sudden changes in the model's behaviour, for which you are not prepared.

There is another obvious advantage in making the early flights under low power and that is, if the model is going to crash, it will crash with rather less violence and damage, if any, will be slighter.

Downthrust may be decreased after a few flights have been made if the model shows no signs of stalling under power. The effect of this will be to bring the nose up under power and the rate of climb will be increased. But remember, you are progressively increasing power which will tend to improve the climb anyway so do not decrease downthrust, or abolish it entirely, until the model has been flown at about full power and the climb seen to be viceless.

But a high rate of climb is not all—particularly with pleasing looking "sport" models, and particularly when your flying space is restricted. There is a tremendous amount of fun to be gained from an aircraft which flies around its launching place and which is pleasing to behold in flight. Long trudges after every flight can be very tiring on a hot afternoon and they will, of course, reduce the number of flights you can make in any one flying session.

CHAPTER 16

Scale models from plastic kits

The author's view is that no thrill in aeromodelling beats the first successful flight of a brand-new model, particularly when you have designed it yourself, as you will if you persist with the hobby. There is, however, a very large and keen body of aeromodellers who assemble non-flying scale models from pre-formed plastic kits. The quality of these kits, generally, is high and the reputable makers, among whom are Airfix, Revell and Frog, achieve remarkable realism and quality in the moulding. Some flying aeromodellers think that plastic kits are just another form of toy requiring no skill, but these are usually people who have never attempted to assemble such a model, especially from a poor kit with inaccurate mouldings, or modify it and finish it in an accurate paint scheme to end up with a replica which would grace any international collection.

Most plastic kits come in recognized scales, the most usual being 1/72nd, 1/48th and 1/96th, the first of these enjoying the greatest popularity. Instructions in most cases are in numbered steps and are easy to follow, but as one gets more experienced they become of secondary importance. Take care when you are assembling a plastic kit to keep the polystyrene cement off the external surface, as this has a bonding quality, eating into the plastic, and it spells disaster for any smooth surface.

Few tools are essential, though the following are useful: a sharp modelling knife, sandpaper, fretsaw blades, a small file, tweezers and, if possible, a number of dentist's instruments for intricate work. All these have proved invaluable to the author.

In some kits "flash" (where waste plastic having oozed from the mould remains fixed as thin flakes to some parts) is prevalent and the trailing edges of the flying surfaces are so thick that, if magnified to their full size, they would be two or three inches thick and would appal professional aerodynamicists, the men responsible for the external shape and the flying qualities of aeroplanes. But these faults can be remedied with care. Excess glue is best left to dry and then sanded after the two parts are firmly cemented, as this will give a cleaner joint. When the larger parts of the model are joined, such as wings and tail to fuselage, and engines to wings, quite large gaps sometimes result. These can be filled with plastic metal which gives a good finish, and a product called Humbrol Putty is specially produced for this purpose. Ordinary household putty is not recommended. The poor man's method consists of mixing plastic shavings and polystyrene cement, which are stirred together until gooey, spread over the crack and sanded when dry.

Modifications and extra details can be made from the plastic stalks to which the pre-formed parts are lightly attached, or from odd pieces of scrap which accumulate after a number of models have been built. These odd extras help to add realistic "clutter" to exposed cockpits or open bomb-bays. Interior details provided usually include pilots, seats and instrument panels, but radios, ammunition boxes, controls and other details of the real machine are often forgotten, but can be made by the painstaking modeller. But remember, when a transparent cockpit canopy is fitted in the closed position some details become hidden from view. To put them in results in wasted time and work.

Minute surface details are often moulded into present kits, so precise has plastic moulding become. Many modellers try to preserve much of this detail but find that by the time one or two coats of paint have been applied very little can be seen, at least on the smaller scale models. Rivets almost always bring groans from the more experienced modeller, particularly if the original aircraft was flush-riveted, and it is usually worth while to sand these off completely. During this process it is not unusual to scratch the clear canopies or windows, but you can remove these scratches by using a steel-wool pad ("Brillo") very carefully, restoring the transparency to its original condition.

The greatest skill in plastic modelling comes in the painting, for it is the finish which can make or break a model. It is here that time and patience can reward you with a replica of which to be proud. Turpentine, or white spirit, fine brushes and masking tape are the essentials (as well as paint, of course) and a steady hand is the most useful extra. Obtain all the references you can on the aircraft you are making (*Aero Modeller, Flight*, Profile Publications' monographs, *Flying Review International* and the Harborough, Putnam and Ian Allan aviation books are all useful sources). If possible, cross-check colours and markings between two different sources. Two good ranges of paints are manufactured by Airfix and Humbrol; these can be intermixed. Both companies do both gloss and matt finishes.

Having applied the basic colours and the transfers supplied with the kit it is worth while to add those extra touches of realism which will separate your model from the mass. No real aircraft remains for long in the gleaming state in which it first emerges from the manufacturer's paintshop. Like everything else it becomes soiled with use. Engines mean soot—and you can add realism by smudging, very carefully, black paint from the exhaust stubs down the fuselage or engine cowlings. Only a small amount is needed so don't overdo it: a photograph of an operational machine is a useful guide. If a camouflaged model of an all-metal aircraft is being built, wear on the wing, nose and tailplane can be shown by small spots of silver paint on the top colour.

Access panels are sometimes outlined in yellow or red and these, painted carefully with the help of masking tape, all help to give realism to what may otherwise be a rather ordinary model. Oil smudges can be simulated around and behind radial engines. On the undersides of the aircraft and on the tyres brown paint, simulating mud, gives the actual appearance of operations from wartime earth strips or peacetime grass fields. There are many other ways of "dirtying up" plastic models to look like the real thing—a touch of red on the exhausts, sooty black around gun muzzles, dull matt red for fabric patches, and silver spots for where wing walkaways and access panels become worn. Whenever you are close to a full-size aircraft study it closely for wear, dirt and other signs of use, and notice particularly how hail and rain erode the paint away from the nose, and the leading edges of the flying surfaces, and how the undercarriage throws up mud on the underside. With these effects retained in your mind's eye, you will find the process of finishing plastic scale models more challenging, but more satisfying when done well.

CHAPTER 17

Some words of advice

With a successful powered free-flight model to your credit, you will have progressed a long way since the day you bought your first kit. Certainly you will by now be used to thinking for yourself where model aircraft are concerned and the author has taken you as far as he is able in this slim book. You may have acquired a preference for one type of flying over another—or you may be raring to tackle other classes of models not touched upon in this book, in particular, control line models which fly around you, tethered by two threads or steel wires through which you can make them climb and dive. Control line flying has its own specialized fields; stunting, racing, combat (where mock dogfights between two or three aircraft are staged) and so on.

But whether you are bitten by the control line bug, or are a convinced glider man, or like free-flight power models to the exclusion of all others, or whether you do not wish to specialize but enjoy all models so long as they *fly*, you will benefit from meeting and flying with other enthusiasts.

There are several hundred model aircraft clubs throughout Great Britain and it is probable that there is one near your home. There may, of course, be an active aeromodellers' club at your school. Some of these clubs specialize in particular branches of aeromodelling but most are comprised of aeromodellers building and flying every kind of model— although quite often a particular craze will sweep through a club and one activity will predominate for some months before giving way to another.

Most clubs give a friendly reception to young and inexperienced aeromodellers. The individual members, particularly the adults, are usually most willing to help a junior with his hobby, and there is an immense amount you can learn from experienced enthusiasts. Plans, materials, engines, are all often freely exchanged; clubs organize week-end flying outings, often with transport arranged, to a distant but extensive flying field or to a rally where members of many clubs meet, to fly both in competition and strictly for fun. Many clubs have a particular arrangement with a local landowner for the use of a flying field which is not generally available. On every score, you will benefit by joining.

The time and meeting place of the local club, and the address of its secretary, are usually known at your local model shop and you are likely to find members congregating there, particularly on Saturday mornings. If you do not establish contact with a club this way, you can obtain particulars of your nearest club by writing to the aeromodellers' national association, the Society of Model Aeronautical Engineers, 10A Electric Avenue, London, S.W.9, enclosing a stamped addressed envelope for the reply.

It is time, too, for you to begin reading the specialist magazine *Aero Modeller*, if you do not already do so and if you intend to proceed further with this absorbing hobby. There are numerous other books on the subject, too, which will guide you to more advanced stages than this basic primer is intended to do. *Aero Modeller* is a monthly and in its pages you will find articles of interest and assistance, useful hints and tips, guidance on flight theory, news of clubs and competitions and of all the latest developments in materials, kits, engines and other equipment. This journal runs a plans service, and adds one or two to its range each month, while there is a full-size pull-out working plan usually included in each issue too. Some of these models will be very advanced, some of average difficulty and some will be very simple.

With the knowledge and aeromodelling wisdom that this journal has to impart, and all the useful tips you can obtain from experienced modellers to add to your own experience, you are well launched in an absorbing hobby.

You can become an expert yourself!